The role of his Book
in Black Hx + am
culture –
And correlated   Ellison
      authors – Washington Dub
      Douglass Hughes
6.50   TN

Richard Wright's
Black Boy (American Hunger)   all the kinds.

A CASEBOOK

– look @ hunger
– freedom literacy
– how the oppressed
   learn oppression
– religion as 'trap'

– Signifying p.187

– 'tension'
– Black Peasant

– Critique of <u>all</u>
   institutions
      – family | not govt
      – church | ~ police
      – school
      – business

Social
Psychology

CASEBOOKS IN CRITICISM

General Editor, William L. Andrews

RICHARD WRIGHT'S

Black Boy (American Hunger)

◆ ◆ ◆

A CASEBOOK

Edited by
William L. Andrews
Douglas Taylor

OXFORD
UNIVERSITY PRESS

2003

OXFORD
UNIVERSITY PRESS

Oxford   New York

Auckland   Bangkok   Buenos Aires   Cape Town   Chennai
Dar es Salaam   Delhi   Hong Kong   Istanbul   Karachi   Kolkata
Kuala Lumpur   Madrid   Melbourne   Mexico City   Mumbai   Nairobi
São Paulo   Shanghai   Taipei   Tokyo   Toronto

Copyright © 2003 by Oxford University Press, Inc.

Published by Oxford University Press, Inc.
198 Madison Avenue, New York, New York 10016

www.oup.com

Oxford is a registered trademark of Oxford University Press

Library of Congress Cataloging-in-Publication Data
Richard Wright's Black boy (American hunger) : a casebook / edited by
William L. Andrews [and] Douglas Taylor.
p. cm. — (Casebooks in criticism)
Includes bibliographical references.
ISBN 0-19-515771-0; 0-19-515772-9 (pbk.)
1. Wright, Richard, 1908–1960. Black boy.   2. Authors,
American—Biography—History and criticism.   3. Wright, Richard,
1908–1960—Contributions in autobiography.   4. African American
authors—Biography—History and criticism.   5. African American
youth—Biography—History and criticism.   6. Wright, Richard,
1908–1960—Childhood and youth.   7. Autobiography.   I. Andrews, William L.,
1946–   II. Taylor, Douglas Edward.   III. Series
PS3545.R815 Z823 2003
813'.52—dc21   2002015616

1 3 5 7 9 8 6 4 2

Printed in the United States of America
on acid-free paper

Credits

Timothy Adams, "Richard Wright: Wearing the Mask," in his *Telling Lies in Modern American Autobiography* (Chapel Hill: University of North Carolina Press, 1990), pp. 69–83. Copyright © 1990 by University of North Carolina Press. Used by permission of the publisher.

Charles T. Davis, "From Experience to Eloquence: Richard Wright's *Black Boy* as Art," in *Chant of Saints,* ed. Robert Stepto and Michael S. Harper (Urbana: University of Illinois Press, 1979), pp. 425–39. Reprinted by permission.

W. E. B. Du Bois, "Richard Wright Looks Back," *New York Herald Tribune,* 4 March 1945, p. 2. Reprinted by permission.

Ralph Ellison, "Richard Wright's Blues," *Antioch Review* 5 (Summer 1945): 198–211. Copyright © 1945 by Antioch Review, Inc. (renewed 1972). First appeared in *Antioch Review* 5, no. 2. Reprinted by permission of the editors.

Yoshinobu Hakutani, "Creation of the Self in Richard Wright's *Black Boy,*" *Black American Literature Forum* 19, no. 2 (Summer 1985):

Contents

Introduction   3
WILLIAM L. ANDREWS AND DOUGLAS TAYLOR

Part I Interview

This, Too, Is America   25
CHARLES J. ROLO

Part II Contemporary Critical Responses

Richard Wright Looks Back: Harsh, Forbidding Memories of
Negro Childhood and Youth   33
W. E. BURGHARDT DU BOIS

A Tragic Situation   37
LIONEL TRILLING

Portrait of a Typical Negro?   41
MARY MCCARTHY

Richard Wright's Blues   45
RALPH ELLISON

Part III Scholarly and Critical Assessments

The Metamorphosis of Richard Wright's *Black Boy*   63
JANICE THADDEUS

From Experience to Eloquence: Richard Wright's
Black Boy as Art   81
CHARLES T. DAVIS

Literacy and Ascent: Richard Wright's *Black Boy*   101
ROBERT B. STEPTO

An Apprenticeship to Life and Art: Narrative Design in Wright's
Black Boy   113
JOHN O. HODGES

Creation of the Self in Richard Wright's *Black Boy*   131
YOSHINOBU HAKUTANI

"Shouting Curses": The Politics of "Bad" Language in Richard
Wright's *Black Boy*   149
JENNIFER H. POULOS

Richard Wright: "Wearing the Mask"   171
TIMOTHY ADAMS

The Horror and the Glory: Richard Wright's Portrait of the
Artist in *Black Boy* and *American Hunger*   191
HORACE A. PORTER

Suggested Reading   209

Richard Wright's
Black Boy (American Hunger)

A CASEBOOK

Introduction

WILLIAM L. ANDREWS
DOUGLAS TAYLOR

◆　◆　◆

RICHARD WRIGHT'S *Black Boy (American Hunger): A Record of Childhood and Youth* (1991) was recently named by Modern Library as one of the top twenty nonfiction works of the twentieth century. When the original edition of *Black Boy* was published in 1945 by Harper and Brothers, critics and scholars alike hailed the book as a major contribution to American as well as African-American autobiography. *Black Boy* became the first African-American autobiography to be listed as a Book-of-the-Month Club selection, testifying to its popular reception in the United States. Rising to first place on the *New York Times* bestseller list, *Black Boy* attracted favorable reviews from a large number of national magazines and was translated into many European languages. It has remained in print since its original publication. The autobiography has been the subject of scholarly articles by critics of American literature, African-American literature, and autobiography studies, and it continues to be one of the most frequently assigned texts in college and university literature courses.

Although Wright was sometimes skeptical about, if not suspicious of, the uses to which mainstream literary, educational, or political institutions put his work, he was glad to see his autobiography taken as seriously as it was by literary critics and social pundits. Even when *Black Boy* was attacked by those whom Wright had knowingly offended, including Communists, large portions of the black middle class and the black intelligentsia, and innumerable southern politicians and social conservatives, Wright did not flinch. He felt he had a responsibility to himself and to the young black men he had grown up with, "the voiceless Negro boys" of the South, to whom, Wright stated in an interview a month after *Black Boy* was published, he felt bound in a kind of spiritual kinship. His aim, he went on in the interview, was "to render a judgment on my environment" so that America would understand that "the environment the South creates is too small to nourish human beings, especially Negro human beings." Though he had managed to survive and transcend the strangling social environment of segregation, Wright considered his success "a matter of luck." "It should be a matter of plan," he insisted. "Not until the sun ceases to shine on you will I disown you," Wright promised the black boys of his youth in the South, of whom he considered himself an "ordinary" representative (Kinnamon and Fabre, 64–65). Through a distinctly extraordinary perspective on growing up in the South, Wright's literary art enabled him to transmute his story of a black boy's personal alienation into a generation's quest for fulfillment and meaning in the modern world.

Richard Wright was born on 24 September 1908 in Roxie, Mississippi, a small town two miles east of Natchez. His mother, Ella Wilson Wright, was a schoolteacher. His father, Nathan, was a tenant farmer who abandoned his family when Richard was six years old. Wright's childhood was marked by frequent migration as a result of the financial difficulties his mother faced as a single parent. At different times during his youth, Wright lived in Memphis, Tennessee; Jackson, Mississippi; Elaine, Arkansas; and Greenwood, Mississippi. While living with his Seventh Day Adventist grandmother in Greenwood, Wright learned the power of literacy from a young schoolteacher who whispered to him the story of

Bluebeard and his seven wives. Wright describes this turning point in his autobiography:

> As her words fell upon my ears, I endowed them with a reality that welled up from somewhere within me. . . . The tale made the world around me be, throb, live. As she spoke, reality changed, the look of things altered, and the world became peopled with magical presences. My sense of life deepened and the feel of things was different, somehow. . . . My imagination blazed. The sensations the story aroused in me were never to leave me. (*Black Boy*, 38–39)

From this point on, Wright embarked on a quest for literacy and self-expression through reading and writing. At thirteen, he took a job as a paperboy in Jackson, Mississippi, to get access to serialized fiction in the newspapers. By age fourteen, he had become an avid reader of pulp fiction in *Flynn's Detective Weekly* and the *Argosy All-Story Magazine*. In the eighth grade he authored a short story, "The Voodoo of Hell's Half-Acre," and gave it to a puzzled editor of a black weekly in Jackson for publication. After moving to Memphis in 1925, he diversified his reading regimen with well-established magazines of literature and culture, such as *Harper's, Atlantic Monthly*, and *American Mercury*.

Wright's desire to learn more about H. L. Mencken, the controversial editor of *American Mercury*, led him to undertake the most ingenious and daring ruse of his literary education. Because African Americans were prohibited from borrowing books from Memphis's public library, Wright forged a letter to the librarian that read, "Dear Madam: Will you please let this nigger boy have some books by H. L. Mencken?" Believing that Wright could not possibly have been the author of the letter because of its use of the word "nigger," the librarian gave Wright a copy of Mencken's *A Book of Prefaces*. This book inspired in Wright an image of the writer he wanted to be, a literary fighter who, the author of *Black Boy* recalled, seemed adept at "using words as a weapon." Exposure to Mencken's work led to encounters with such important American and European fiction writers as Fyodor Dostoyevsky, Gustave

Flaubert, Leo Tolstoy, Mark Twain, Stephen Crane, Émile Zola, Maxim Gorky, Edgar Allan Poe, Sherwood Anderson, Sinclair Lewis, Frank Norris, and Theodore Dreiser. The hunger for new knowledge aroused from such reading impelled Wright to leave the South in December 1927. He was nineteen years old.

In Chicago, despite frequent unemployment and a series of low-paying temporary jobs, Wright pursued his dream of a literary career, publishing an early story, "Superstition," in a local African-American periodical, *Abbott's Monthly Magazine*, in April 1931. Scarcely two years later he became an active member of the John Reed Club, a front organization for the Communist party, chiefly because the Chicago branch of the club sponsored a literary magazine, *Left Front*, that encouraged submissions from Wright. During the mid-1930s Wright published several articles and poems in various Communist and left-leaning magazines. Wright's best-known poem from this period was "Between the World and Me," published in the July–August 1935 issue of *Partisan Review*. The poem describes the narrator's encounter with the charred remains of a lynching victim. Wright's most important essay from this period was "Blueprint for Negro Writing" (1937), an aesthetic manifesto that signaled his break from the artistic pretensions and middle-class values that he found prevalent among earlier African-American writers. But Wright's first success as a fiction writer came with the publication of *Uncle Tom's Children* in 1938. The first edition of *Uncle Tom's Children* was composed of four novellas: "Big Boy Leaves Home," "Fire and Cloud," "Down by the Riverside," and "Long Black Song." Later editions would include an autobiographical essay entitled "The Ethics of Living Jim Crow" and a fifth story, "Bright and Morning Star." Each of the novellas in *Uncle Tom's Children* deals with acts of resistance and survival by African Americans living under the racist restrictions of the Jim Crow South. *Uncle Tom's Children* was well received by most critics and led to Wright winning the 1938 *Story Magazine* prize for the best book written by a writer involved with the Federal Writers' Project. A year later Wright was awarded a prestigious Guggenheim fellowship because of his new book, a development that allowed him to leave his job at the U.S. Post

Office and work full time on a book he insisted would be "so hard and deep that [readers] would have to face it without the consolation of tears" ("How Bigger Was Born," introduction to Harper-Perennial edition of *Native Son*, p. xxvii). That book was *Native Son* (1940), the novel that secured Wright's lasting fame as a major American author.

Native Son portrays the short, violent life of Bigger Thomas, a product of Chicago's black ghetto, who inadvertently becomes a murderer and, after a citywide manhunt, is tried and convicted for his crime. In the final part of the novel, as he awaits execution, Bigger reflects on his horrific career in dialogues with his lawyer, which give him insight into the forces that created him, while allowing his creator to speak to his readership frankly and ominously about the wages of American racism. Summing up the meaning of his life in a perverse revision of the Cartesian *cogito ergo sum*, Bigger claims, "What I killed for, I *am!*"

Despite its shocking subject matter and tough-minded approach to social evils in urban America, *Native Son* sold 200,000 copies within three weeks of its publication. Selected by the Book-of-the-Month Club, the novel became a bestseller while enjoying overwhelmingly positive reviews from literary critics. *Native Son* was adapted for the stage and produced on Broadway with Orson Welles as director. It also served as the basis for two films: *Sangre Negra* (1950) and *Native Son* (1986). Produced in Argentina and directed by Pierre Chenal, *Sangre Negra* stars Wright himself as Bigger Thomas. The 1986 film adaptation of the novel stars Oprah Winfrey as Bigger's mother and Matt Dillon as Mary's boyfriend, Jan, with a relative newcomer to film, Victor Love, in the lead role. Though neither movie was successful at the box office, *Native Son* remains one of the most influential African-American novels of the twentieth century

Wright's next book, *Twelve Million Black Voices* (1941), offers a photographic history of African Americans living in the rural South and industrial North of the United States. The book presents a scathing indictment of America's political and economic disfranchisement of its black citizens. Indeed, federal authorities in Washington, D.C., considered Wright's commentary so damning that they opened a file on him as a possible subversive whose activities and publications needed to be monitored. Among these activities may have been the train ride Wright took to Nashville, Tennessee, in the spring of 1943 at the behest of the noted African-American sociologist Charles Johnson, who had invited Wright to give a talk at Fisk University. After enduring travel in a Jim Crow car through Tennessee, during which he witnessed the self-effacement and false humility in black passengers' inter-actions with whites, Wright spoke at length on 9 April to his Fisk audience about his own experiences in the South.

His theme was the climate of discrimination that had circum-scribed his existence as a boy and molded him into the man he had become. In a newspaper article published more than a year after his visit to Fisk, Wright recalled the responses of whites and blacks alike to his talk:

> There was but little applause. Indeed, the audience was terribly still, and it was not until I was halfway through my speech that it crashed upon me that I was saying things that Negroes were not supposed to say publicly, things that whites had for-bidden. What made me realize this was a hysterical, half-repressed, tense kind of laughter that went up now and then from the white and black faces. (Fabre 249)

Prior to this trip, Wright had been working on a novel. But after this unsettling return to his homeland thrust him back into the past, Wright put fiction aside to devote his full attention to au-tobiography. He finished the first draft in only eight months. Not merely a personal story, Wright's autobiography was designed to blur the boundaries between sociology and autobiography by con-veying not only the complexity of Wright's personal experience but its applicability to many African-American men's lives in the early twentieth-century South.

When Richard Wright submitted his autobiography to Harper and Brothers in December 1943, it was entitled *American Hunger*. The manuscript consisted of two sections, "Southern Night," which treated Wright's life in the South, and "The Horror and the Glory," which chronicled Wright's experiences in Chicago from his arrival in 1927 to well into the 1930s. To secure selection by the Book-of-the-Month Club, which in turn would ensure substantial sales, Wright agreed in the summer of 1944 to publish only the first section of his autobiography, under the title *Black Boy*. Parts of "The Horror and the Glory" appeared in magazines around the time of *Black Boy*'s publication, but the entire second part of Wright's autobiography as he wrote it in 1943 did not see print until 1977, when Harper and Row published the Chicago section of Wright's original autobiography as *American Hunger*. Not until 1991, when the Library of America published *Black Boy (American Hunger)*, did Wright's complete autobiography as he conceived it and wrote it in the early 1940s finally come into print.

Black Boy (American Hunger) recounts Wright's struggles with family and society as he attempts to define and preserve a sustaining sense of selfhood as a child, an adolescent, and, eventually, an aspiring writer who abandons the segregated South for the quasi freedom and opportunity of the North. The narrative is punctuated by searing memories of alienation and repression: abandonment by his father; poverty and hunger growing up in a single-parent household; harsh discipline meted out by an overzealous, Seventh Day Adventist grandmother; indifference from black friends and family in the South; and suspicion and hostility from white southerners. Yet Wright's imagination flowered through often fortuitous encounters with literature, which provided him intellectual community and emotional nurture until he could make his way from Mississippi to Memphis and ultimately to Chicago.

"The Horror and the Glory," the second part of *Black Boy (American Hunger)*, describes Wright's life in Chicago, where he worked at positions ranging from busboy, ditch digger, and night janitor to postal worker, lecturer, and editor in left-wing literary circles. Most of "The Horror and the Glory" relates Wright's conflicted involvement with the Communist party, of which he was a member for three years, and offers Wright's firsthand account of both the value and limitations of the party's work in urban African-American communities.

As though the retelling of his life freed him to move on to another phase of it, Wright accepted an invitation from the French government in 1946 to come to France. In 1947, Wright, his wife, Ellen, and their daughter, Julia, moved to Paris. He would never return to live in the United States. In France, Wright resumed his career as a novelist, publishing *The Outsider* (1953), *Savage Holiday* (1954), and *The Long Dream* (1958). *The Outsider*, an existentialist thriller, tells the story of Cross Damon, an African-American postal employee and self-educated intellectual who fakes his death in a subway accident so as to escape his family responsibilities and live under an assumed identity outside the constraints of morality and law. *Savage Holiday*, the only novel by Wright in which racial issues are peripheral, centers on the life of a white insurance salesman, Erskine Fowler. The most psychological of all of Wright's novels, *Savage Holiday* explores the way that childhood trauma and repressed desire cause Fowler to destroy himself. *The Long Dream* distinguishes itself from the rest of the novels in Wright's oeuvre by focusing on middle-class African Americans. None of these novels enjoyed the reception, popular or critical, that *Native Son* garnered.

In addition to the novels Wright wrote in France, he also published three travel books: *Black Power* (1954), based on a trip to Ghana on the verge of its independence from Great Britain; *The Color Curtain* (1956), a report on a conference held in Bandung, Indonesia, of twenty-nine newly independent African and Asian nations; and *Pagan Spain* (1957), which surveys Spanish culture from the vantage point of two car trips Wright made to Spain in 1956 and early 1957. In 1957 Wright collected a number of his speeches on national and international aspects of the race question and added an essay on "The Literature of the Negro in the United States" for a volume he titled *White Man, Listen!*

On 28 November 1960, twenty-two years after the publication of his first collection of short stories, Wright died unexpectedly of heart failure at the Eugène Gibez Clinic in Paris. The mysterious circumstances of his death—Wright had been recovering from amoebic dysentery, for which he was being treated at the Gibez clinic; he had no history of heart disease; he died shortly after receiving an injection; and his body was immediately cremated without his family's permission—combined with the fact that he had been the subject of FBI surveillance and harassment since 1942, led many to believe that he may have been the victim of foul play. Letters he wrote to friends and colleagues suggest that Wright himself was concerned (some say, paranoid) about his safety because of his public criticism of U.S. foreign policy in the Third World. However, Michel Fabre, Wright's most respected biographer, stated in 1993:

> In my opinion the CIA would not have shrunk from suppressing a dangerous opponent to their policies, but among Wright's ideological and political activities at the time I could find nothing likely to lead the CIA to consider him dangerous and subversive enough to warrant assassination. The disclosure of the (admittedly heavily censored) FBI dossier about Wright does not suggest that he was under longer or more special surveillance than James Baldwin or Chester Himes. (Fabre xv)

Fabre's observation is in keeping with the fact that, by the end of his life, Wright had alienated himself from many of Paris's black expatriates; his popularity had significantly declined among American readers, black and white, as well.

Since his death, however, Wright's literary reputation has grown and solidified both in the United States and abroad. In the late 1960s and 1970s, the Black Arts movement and many proponents of a black aesthetic championed Wright, praising him for his hard-hitting attacks on American racism and his concern for the African-American underclass. Fiction and poetry that Wright had been unable to publish, in part or whole, during his lifetime has appeared often since his death, indicating an enduring interest in his work. Among Wright's posthumously published fiction are *Eight Men* (1961), a collection of short stories about black men from various class backgrounds and regions who seek to negotiate or extricate themselves from the racial minefield of American society; and *Lawd Today* (1963), a novel Wright wrote before *Native Son*, which explores a day in the life of an African-American postal worker. In 1994, HarperCollins published a young adult novel by Wright entitled *Rite of Passage*, and in 1998, Arcade Publishing under the editorship of Yoshinobu Hakutani and Robert L. Tener brought out a collection of Wright's verse under the title *Haiku: This Other World.* Testifying to the enduring status of Wright's most important work, the Library of America published in 1991 a two-volume edition of restored and complete versions of *Uncle Tom's Children, Native Son, The Outsider,* and *Lawd Today* along with *Black Boy (American Hunger).* By this time the scholarly world had already confirmed the centrality of Wright's contribution to twentieth-century American literature. In 1988 Keneth Kinnamon, one of the most knowledgeable scholar-critics in African-American literature studies, published *A Richard Wright Bibliography,* which, surveying a half century of criticism and commentary on Wright's work, comprises more than 13,000 items. The annual bibliographies of critical work on Wright that appear in the *Richard Wright Newsletter* demonstrate that the author of *Black Boy (American Hunger)* remains one of the most discussed figures in American literature of the twentieth century.

Richard Wright's Black Boy (American Hunger): *A Casebook* presents reviews and critical analyses of the 1945 edition of *Black Boy* and the 1977 edition of *American Hunger,* while also affirming the appreciation of scholars and critics for the restored and complete *Black Boy (American Hunger)* as the now-standard edition of Wright's autobiography. Like most of the books in the Casebooks in Criticism series, this casebook includes an interview with the author himself. In May 1945, Wright's comments on the recently published *Black Boy* appeared in a review of the book written by Charles J. Rolo, a white literary journalist who later reviewed Wright's work for the *Atlantic* and the *Saturday Review of Literature.* Rolo admired Wright and his autobiography and was untroubled, though writing at the outset of the Cold War, by Wright's assertion that "the artist is a revolutionary figure." What Rolo seems most concerned with in the interview is not probing the resources of Wright's art but extracting sociopolitical pronouncements from him about the "solution to the Negro problem." Wright's responses to Rolo's questions illuminate the black writer's thinking about issues pertinent to his own life, such as migration from the South, and his views of white literary crusaders against racism. The edginess and reserve that Rolo attributes to Wright—characteristics that seem to have affected Wright's willingness to reveal himself to almost all of his interviewers—may well have been due as much to his uneasiness with playing the racial spokesperson for black America as to the divided self that Rolo ascribes to Wright at the end of their interview.

While Wright may have been ambivalent about assuming the role of spokesperson, others were less willing to allow him to dispense with this responsibility. In "Richard Wright Looks Back," one of several reviews in the Contemporary Critical Responses section of this casebook, W. E. B. Du Bois, the most important African-American scholar of the twentieth century, berates Wright for failing to maintain in *Black Boy* a level of bourgeois decency and decorum, which Wright himself had thoroughly rejected years earlier in his essay "Blueprint for Negro Writing." Disturbed by the blending of fact and fiction, personal account and historical record in *Black Boy*, Du Bois systematically critiques Wright's portrayal of each of the autobiography's major "characters" and claims that Wright misjudged both blacks and whites by rendering almost all of his "characters" repulsive and detestable. Du Bois further criticizes Wright for slipping into the mode of "commentator and prophet" in the authoritative (and generally negative) pronouncements he makes about African-American culture in *Black Boy*. Although Du Bois never says as much directly, he seems concerned that Wright's negative portrayal of black southern culture will provide ammunition for white racists. Insistent upon always putting the best foot forward for the African-American community he devoted his life to serving, Du Bois ends his review by stating: "Nothing that Richard Wright says is in itself unbelievable or impossible; it is the total picture that is not convincing."

Lionel Trilling's "A Tragic Situation" applauds the integrity Wright demonstrates as a writer by not allowing his readers what Trilling describes as a "moral escape." Anticipating James Baldwin's critique of protest literature in his essay "Everybody's Protest

Novel," Trilling suggests that the dangers of protest literature are providing readers with a zone of safety from which they can observe the suffering of others without feeling any need to help alleviate that suffering; encouraging feelings of false superiority to the one-dimensional villains who people the pages of protest books; and inspiring in some readers a kind of primitivist sentimentality, which considers virtue or wisdom to be the natural outcome of misery and suffering. All of these facile responses to protest writing tend to undermine the efforts of reformers to eliminate the causes of the suffering being protested. Trilling suggests that *Black Boy* avoids these traps because Wright, as both author and protagonist, is able to achieve enough distance from his subject matter that readers are unable to conceive of him in stereotypical fashion as a suffering, victimized Other but are rather forced to recognize in *Black Boy*'s protagonist a sense of agency and complexity not altogether different from their own.

Mary McCarthy's "Portrait of a Typical Negro?" responds to a question that plagued many white readers as they encountered *Black Boy* for the first time, namely, are the thoughts and emotions of Wright's protagonist representative of the thoughts and emotions of black Americans in general? As naïve as this question may sound to twenty-first-century readers, it was one that Wright partially encouraged by claiming that, in writing *Black Boy*, he wanted to "lend, give [his] tongue to the voiceless Negro boys" of the South. A variation of this question also formed the basis of the objections posed by many of the book's black critics, namely, that Richard was *not* representative of "the Negro," the implication being that Wright had a responsibility to present white readers with African-American characters and protagonists who were more typical. McCarthy suggests that white readers cannot allow themselves to believe that *Black Boy*'s protagonist is in any way representative of a larger population of African Americans, because to do so would be to admit that the little interaction they did have with blacks, though seemingly friendly and courteous, was actually based on a lie. To accept the thought and experiences of Wright's black boy as typical of that of the overwhelming majority of black boys growing up in the South would be to acknowledge that most blacks resented whites for the racism that confined much of their daily existence and that they were justified in feeling this resentment. Unfortunately, as if proving her own thesis, McCarthy spends the second part of her review psychoanalyzing Wright in such a way as to suggest that Wright, more than likely out of a neurotic need to differentiate himself from those by whom he was surrounded, provoked the greater part of the racial and familial conflict that he records in his autobiography.

Ralph Ellison's essay-length review, "Richard Wright's Blues," like Du Bois's "Richard Wright Looks Back," offers some insight into how *Black Boy* was received by African-American critics. But more important, Ellison's review also provides readers with the reactions and scholarly assessment of a friend (Ellison was the best man in Wright's first wedding), a protégé, and the author of *Invisible Man* (1952), a book many critics consider the most important American novel of the post–World War II era. In "Richard Wright's Blues," Ellison argues that in addition to the influence of autobiographies and autobiographical novels such as Jawaharlal Nehru's *Toward Freedom* (1941), James Joyce's *Portrait of the Artist as a Young Man* (1915), and Fyodor Dostoyevsky's *The House of the Dead* (translated into English in 1931), *Black Boy* is deeply indebted to the blues. Indeed, Ellison views *Black Boy*, as he would later consider *Invisible Man*, as a fruitful combination of "high" art and "low" art, canonical literature and African-American oral folk expression. Accordingly, Ellison differs from the other reviewers in this casebook in his insistence that, as bleak as Wright's vision of black life in the South may be, it is not without beauty, hope, or humor. Ellison argues that Wright, like the blues balladeers who helped to inspire him, recounts a tale of suffering and woe not merely to elicit pity from his readers but so that they might find ways to transcend that suffering as part of their common quest to achieve a more democratic society.

The initial essay in the Scholarly and Critical Assessments section of this casebook is Janice Thaddeus's "The Metamorphosis of Richard Wright's *Black Boy*." Thaddeus's study of the entire text of Wright's autobiography, both before and after it was split up, allows us to see the unity of mood, design, and purpose in Wright's autobiography as he originally wrote it. Thaddeus also provides valuable information on Wright's motives for cutting his autobiography in half. This essay also calls attention to the ways Wright revised his original autobiography to create the 1945 version of *Black Boy*, in particular by adding a conclusion to that version that the original text did not contain. Arguing compellingly that the 1945 version of *Black Boy* was "truncated" and not reflective of "the lack of conviction" and "the isolation" that Wright's complete autobiography communicated, Thaddeus urges her readers, as do the editors of this casebook, to base their judgments of the work on the text that reprints the entirety of Wright's autobiography, in other words, on *Black Boy (American Hunger)*.

By the time Thaddeus published her 1985 essay, four decades of critical analysis and scholarship had been devoted to the 1945 *Black Boy*. Some of the most important studies of *Black Boy* confronted the vexed question of whether the book should be read primarily as a factual record of an individual life or as an artistic rendering of a more or less representative experience. Attempting to bring an end to the conflict between Du Bois's critique of *Black Boy* and Ellison's defense of the text, Charles T. Davis, in his 1979 essay "From Experience to Eloquence: Richard Wright's *Black Boy* as Art," argues that, for the literary critic, what is more important than ferreting out the truth or falsity of Wright's representation of black life in the South is determining the governing principles of Wright's art. Davis endeavors to do this by comparing the life Wright lived, as it has been unearthed by Michel Fabre in his landmark biography, *The Unfinished Quest of Richard Wright*, with the life he narrates in *Black Boy*. Davis argues that the text's narrator speaks in three voices. The first voice describes the development of the narrator's emotional vocabulary as he passes from one traumatic childhood experience to another. The second voice charts the development of Wright's literary imagination against the harsh backdrop of the Jim Crow South. The third voice, according to Davis, is a didactic voice that occasionally interrupts the flow of the narrative to offer "sociological" explanations for the events the two other voices describe.

Robert Stepto's "Literacy and Ascent: Richard Wright's *Black Boy*" examines the ways that *Black Boy* completes Wright's earlier novel, *Native Son*, by providing a literary answer to the seemingly extraliterary question of how Wright escaped the fate of a character like Bigger Thomas, given similar circumstances of birth and upbringing. True to his claim that this question "need not be answered . . . in a nonliterary way," Stepto does not look for a response in the historical details of Wright's life (not even as Wright artistically reinterpreted them in *Black Boy*). Instead, Stepto seeks an answer to this question in instances of textual consonance and dissonance both within *Black Boy* and between *Black Boy* and other related texts within the African-American tradition. Out of this intertextual play of differences, Stepto reconstructs Wright's unique path toward literacy and freedom within the context of other canonical narratives, such as Frederick Douglass's *Narrative of the Life of Frederick Douglass* (1845), James Weldon Johnson's *Autobiography of an Ex-Colored Man* (1912), and Wright's own *Native Son*. Stepto's cogent comparative analysis demonstrates how the quest for literacy Wright so eloquently describes in *Black Boy* ultimately led to his emancipation from a fate he might have shared with Bigger Thomas, his most famous literary creation.

John Hodges's "An Apprenticeship to Life and Art: Narrative Design in Wright's *Black Boy*" looks at *Black Boy* as a *Bildungsroman*, or novel of education. Like Ellison, Hodges locates Wright's autobiography in a European tradition that includes such works as Goethe's *Wilhelm Meister* (1796), Keller's *Grune Hëinrich* (1880), and Joyce's *Portrait of the Artist as a Young Man*. However, unlike these classic *Bildungsromaner*, Hodges argues, *Black Boy* concerns both a young man's coming of age in a restrictive society and his confronting social and political alienation in a racially oppressive southern caste system. *Black Boy* also differs from the classic *Bildungsroman* by treating Wright's life as representative of the lives of the many other young black men of his peer group and generation. These divergences from the conventions of the traditional

Bildungsroman are due to what Hodges argues are the two purposes of the text: to enable Wright to retrace the trajectory of his own life in order to better understand his relationship to the African-American community and to indict southern whites for impeding the hopes and aspirations of black youth. It is the second of these two objectives, Hodges argues, that leads Wright to embody such hope and aspiration in *Black Boy*'s naïve protagonist. By presenting readers with a protagonist who appears bewildered by the southern caste system in which he is immersed, Wright forced blacks and whites to question anew a set of social relations that the least hopeful and most apathetic had come to view as inevitable.

In "Creation of the Self in Richard Wright's *Black Boy*," Yoshinobu Hakutani maintains that *Black Boy*, rather than being read as "A Record of Childhood and Youth," is best understood as fiction or fictionalized autobiography. Hakutani supports this claim by echoing Davis, who notes discrepancies between events as they occurred in Wright's life and those same events as they appear in *Black Boy*, and Hodges, who stresses Wright's use of the literary conceit of the naïve youth as a means of interrogating the traditions and mores of the segregationist South, thereby giving *Black Boy* a form reminiscent of famous fictional growing-up stories. Hakutani adds more reasons for judging *Black Boy* as a fictionalized autobiography by analyzing the book's impersonal narrative voice and its uncharacteristic (for an autobiography) external focus. Both of these traits, Hakutani suggests, are more commonly associated with the tradition of literary naturalism, which Wright himself acknowledged to be a major influence in his work. Hence, for Hakutani, *Black Boy* is not merely a fictionalized autobiography; it is, more precisely, a naturalistic autobiography, a new kind of writing that uses personal narrative to explore sociological issues.

Jennifer Poulos's " 'Shouting Curses': The Politics of 'Bad' Language in Richard Wright's *Black Boy*" looks at how *Black Boy* uses profanity to up-end social hierarchies and create a space in which Wright expresses himself as an artist free from the negative value judgments of both blacks and whites. Poulos argues that for any black person to acquire the tools of eloquent self-expression was a threat to the racial order erected by southern whites and was therefore, ipso facto, "bad." For blacks concerned with securing their survival within this same system of social relations, free and open expression of thought by any member of their "race" was a threat to every member. Reflecting on Wright's early attempts to find his voice within a society in which any artful, literate use of language by a black person was necessarily considered "bad" language, Poulos argues that Wright metaphorically links the profanity used by various characters in the text with the "bad" language of what, for blacks, was considered socially inappropriate expression. In doing so, Wright effects a revaluation of norms, which transforms "bad" language into "good" and "good" language into "bad."

Timothy Adams's "Richard Wright: 'Wearing the Mask' " offers the best informed and most balanced approach to the long-standing controversy over the authenticity of Wright's representation of black life in the South. Citing Ralph White, a psychologist, who commended Wright for *Black Boy*'s "ruthless honesty," and Du Bois's claim that the book was "unconvincing," Adams steers a middle course by granting validity to both opposing positions. According to Adams, *Black Boy*'s refusal to tell the truth is due to Wright's determination to confront a greater social truth, which the design of the text is intended to convey. Rather than viewing the less convincing moments in *Black Boy* as deliberate attempts to deceive the reader, Adams sees them as intentional renderings of the difficult dilemmas with which black boys growing up under the rigid codes and social conventions of the Jim Crow South were often faced, dilemmas that frequently required them to lie or dissemble in order to survive. Adams further points out that, unlike other autobiographies whose authenticity has been called into question, *Black Boy* does not misrepresent the truth to make Wright seem more admirable or important than he actually was. Wright's manipulation of autobiographical truth aims instead to bring the facts of his life into closer proximity with the archetypal southern black boy on whom the text centers. Like Ellison, who sees *Black Boy*'s alternations between hope and despair as linking it to the African-American folk form of the blues, Adams views *Black Boy* as a complex elaboration of the black vernacular speech genre of the *lie*—a fantastic combination of truth and falsity usually narrated to entertain or illustrate an important social moral or truth. Thus Adams ends his essay with the conclusion that "Du Bois's assessment . . . was exactly backward: although much of what Wright wrote is not literally true, the total picture is ultimately convincing."

In one of the first articles to critically comment on *Black Boy* and *American Hunger* as a single narrative, Horace Porter's "The Horror and the Glory: Richard Wright's Portrait of the Artist in *Black Boy* and *American Hunger*" illustrates Wright's use of the redemptive and transformational power of words to cultivate a unique artistic identity. Like Hodges, who compares *Black Boy* to texts within the continental canon, Porter's points of comparison are with European texts like James Joyce's *Portrait of the Artist as a Young Man*, Jean-Paul Sartre's *Les Mots* (1964), and Thomas Mann's *Tonio Kröger* (1903). Tracing the development of the emotional vocabulary that Davis identified as the main theme of one of the autobiography's three central voices, Porter shows how *Black Boy* links Wright's "banishment" of his father to his acquisition of verbal mastery, and his symbolization of his mother (Wright says that his ailing mother became a symbol of suffering to him) to his decision to dedicate his life's work as an artist to the analysis and alleviation of human suffering. Porter also argues that the punishment Richard receives for his naïve transcription of curse words onto the walls and windows of neighborhood businesses, the vehemence with which his grandmother prohibits him from listening to the tale of Bluebeard and his seven wives, and the perplexity with which the publication of his first short story, "The Voodoo of Hell's Half-Acre," was greeted by relatives and friends impressed Wright with the power and mystery of the written word. The same adventurousness and restless curiosity Wright demonstrated in these childhood incidents would emerge, in the *American Hunger* section of the autobiography, as the very traits responsible for his attraction to and ultimate expulsion from the Communist party.

Much of the criticism of Richard Wright's *Black Boy* *(American Hunger)* focuses on the more formal aspects of the text, interrogating questions of representation, genre, and language. The second most common approach to examining the text has been comparative—analyzing *Black Boy* in relation to Wright's biography, literary antecedents, and the historical record. While scholarship of this nature is crucial to our understanding of Wright's autobiography, other areas of inquiry need to be investigated. Foremost among these are the role of gender and sexuality in the text. All autobiography, to a greater or lesser extent, is engaged in the production of gendered subjects, culturally recognizable masculine or feminine protagonists. There are many questions that scholars and students might begin to ask of *Black Boy*. How is masculinity constructed and portrayed in this autobiography? Considering the physical violence that permeates the book, for example, when young Richard must fight to earn "the right to the streets of Memphis" from boys who attempt to steal his money, or when Richard allows white men to manipulate him into fighting Harrison, a young black man against whom he previously held no grievance, what impact do such experiences have on Wright's sense of African-American manhood? What is the significance of Wright's portrayal of women, especially black women, who so often in *Black Boy* *(American Hunger)* are portrayed as controlling, if not outright oppressive and threatening? What are we to make of Wright's insistent identification of himself as a kind of rugged artist-individualist, who disavows "politics" because it hinders full and free self-expression? In light of the persistent efforts of critics to find a sociopolitical message in *Black Boy* *(American Hunger)*, what does the narrative's critique of "politics" as antithetical to Wright's aim as an artist say about the relationship between art and political work? We hope that this casebook on *Black Boy* *(American Hunger)* will promote continuing study and investigations of questions such as these in light of the revealing routes of inquiry that have already been undertaken into this rich and enduring work of literature.

Works Cited

Fabre, Michel. *The Unfinished Quest of Richard Wright*. 2d. ed. Urbana: University of Illinois Press, 1993.

Kinnamon, Keneth, and Michel Fabre, eds. *Conversations with Richard Wright*. Jackson: University Press of Mississippi, 1993.

Wright, Richard. *Black Boy (American Hunger)*. Edited by Arnold Rampersad. New York: Literary Classics of the United States, 1991.

Part I

◆   ◆   ◆

INTERVIEW

This, Too, Is America

CHARLES J. ROLO

◆　◆　◆

T HE ARTIST IS A REVOLUTIONARY FIGURE," says
Richard Wright. "The serious artist grapples with his environment, passes a judgment on it. He helps to deepen people's
perceptions, quicken their thought processes. He makes them
conscious of the possibility of historical change—and in that way
he facilitates change. That's a big task, a self-sufficient one."

Ten years ago Wright believed that the artist had a role to play
in politics, too. He was active in the John Reed Clubs, the League
of American Writers, and other left-wing organizations. He is convinced now, he says, that the artist is most effective when he
sticks to his trade. "Writers and politicians move in a different
tempo, on a different plane. Let the politician organize what the
writer has set in motion. When a writer starts dabbling in politics,
he gets sucked into an organization that amounts to leaving his
work. He should put all of his passion into his work."

Richard Wright has done just that. All of his passion, all of
his indignation against the Jim Crow system, the third-class citi-
zenship, and the *Sklavenmoral* imposed on the American Negro he

has put into a courageous, heartbreaking, sordid, explosive, sometimes melodramatic, but unforgettable book, *Black Boy*.

Black Boy is an autobiography, a document in race relations, and a moral indictment; it combines the unashamed subjectivity of Rousseau's *Confessions* with the harsh realism of Zola's *L'Assomoir* and the crusading fervor of his *J'accuse*. The tension, the bitterness, the tragedy are unrelieved, unshaded. It could hardly have been otherwise, for tension and hate and gray hopelessness were the realities of this black boy's story, which is also the story of America's lower depths.

Some reviewers have complained about Wright's "strained and feverish" manner; to their air-conditioned idealism the violence of his style is like a jet of steam from a burst pipe. "The manner," Wright says:

> stems from the matter; the relationship of the American Negro to the American scene is essentially violent. He could not be kept in his present position unless there existed an apparatus of organized violence. Any attempt to deal with this situation must deal in terms of violence. I cannot deny the reality of my existence. It's what I've seen.

Richard Wright was born on a plantation near Natchez and grew up in the slums of Memphis and the small-town slums of Arkansas and Mississippi. When Richard was five, his father deserted his mother. A few years later his mother was crippled by paralysis. His childhood was a nightmare of abject poverty, hunger, and fear—poverty that sent him begging for pennies in the saloons, where the grown-ups would get him drunk and give him nickels to repeat obscenities; hunger that was forever "nudging my ribs, twisting my empty guts until they ached"; fear of the beatings at home, of hostile black children, of ghosts, and of the harsh religion of his grandmother—and, later, dread of the white world, which murdered his uncle and lynched a boyhood acquaintance, in which the slightest slip of word or expression meant ugly trouble.

The underprivileged black boy was by instinct a rebel, with a burning sense of the dignity of man. In the black world as well as the white he remained a stranger and alone. Even his uncle told the other children to keep away from him—"the boy's a dangerous fool." His white employers, too, sensed that he was "different"—though he learned to say "sir," smile with false heartiness, and mask his thoughts and feelings. "I don't like your looks, nigger," one man said, and fired him. He was run off job after job.

He saw the worst side of the white man's world. When a dog bit him, its owner laughed: a dog bite can't hurt a nigger. "If I was a nigger," one boss said to him, "I'd kill myself." The foreman in an optical factory gave him and another black boy knives and tried to incite a stabbing. As a bellboy in a hotel he grew used to seeing white prostitutes lolling naked on their beds—blacks were supposed to take nakedness for granted; they were not considered human.

Richard Wright found his first release in the printed word. When he was a small boy, a schoolteacher read to him the story of *Bluebeard and His Seven Wives*, and as she spoke, "the look of things was different, and the world became peopled with magic presences. My sense of life deepened and the feel of things was different, somehow." His grandmother beat him—any non-Bible story was the Devil's work—and told him he would burn in hell. But he had tasted "what to me was life," and thereafter he would slip into the schoolteacher's room, steal a book, and try to decipher it in the barn. At thirteen he had not yet had an unbroken year of schooling, but he was reading everything he could lay his hands on—cheap pulp tales, for the most part, in the magazine supplement of a Ku Klux Klan paper. At fourteen he had his first story published in a Negro newspaper; he called it "The Voodoo of Hell's Half-Acre." Three years later a friendly Irishman lent him a library card, and he discovered H. L. Mencken, Sherwood Anderson, and Sinclair Lewis. Their books were his "gateway to the world." For the first time he learned that white men were fighting prejudice and stupidity and shams, using words as one would use a club, and instinctively he thought: "Maybe I could use words as a weapon." He bought a ream of paper and started to write.

The miracle of Richard Wright's achievement can no more be explained than Beethoven's genius or the poetic gift of Rimbaud in his teens. *Black Boy* certainly fails to account for the miracle, and Richard Wright has just this to add: "Some people see a ballgame and they want to play ball; some see water and they want to swim; when I saw print, I wanted to write."

Why didn't he turn out like his own Bigger Thomas, for violence and crime were the norm of his early days?

"Well, for one thing," says Wright, "I kept out of jail; I never got caught. And when I had enough money to start north, I never stole again."

Wright does not believe that migration to the North is a solution to the Negro problem. But when the southern Negro goes north, he tears himself loose from folk-peasant ways, becomes urbanized—and in that, Wright sees a measure of salvation for the Negro:

> Urbanization brings the southern Negro within the living orbit of the nation for the first time. It brings him into contact with literacy, with democratic ideas, makes him conscious of his relation to the nation.
>
> The war has accelerated the northward drift, and has speeded up the progress of the Negro. But it has been an unconscious process—like an express train stirring up dry leaves. What is needed is conscious acceleration. In Mississippi, for instance, the state spends $40 a year on the education of a white child, $5 a year on the education of a Negro child. If the Negro child is to overcome his cultural handicaps, he needs $60 or $80 a year.

The war, too, says Wright:

> has shown up the fallacy of the old slogan "There's nothing wrong with the South but what jobs wouldn't cure." Today

there are plenty of jobs, but the southerner's attitude toward the Negro has not improved. What the Negro wants is not just a job but the rights granted by the Constitution. That problem will be decided by hard factual thinking—not by paltry economic concessions, made by way of appeasement, or by moral paternalism. There's a danger in riding the moral horse. The well-meaning old ladies who say nice things about "my nice colored maid" are sidestepping the Negro problem.

Although white liberals have done much to improve the status of the Negro, Wright is not too hopeful that mass pressure for racial equality will be exerted on the South by whites. According to a recent survey, Wright says, 60 percent of the whites in America believe that the Negro is being fairly treated. The Negro, he is convinced, will have to assume the initiative.

What of the white writers crusading for the Negro?

Their motives are admirable, but often their point of attack is mistaken. There's no need for them to make special pleas to the Negro to increase his militancy. The militancy is there, spilling over. Their task, as I conceive it, is to grapple with the deep-seated racial notions of white Americans. Lillian Smith is one who sees this quite clearly and addresses her work to her own class. White writers should combat white chauvinism while Negro writers combat Negro nationalism and chronic distrust of the whites. Negro nationalism—the all-black community—spells social regression. There is no solution in withdrawal; withdrawal means perishing. The Negro has no culture except the culture of the rest of the country. As I see it, integration—complete equality—is the only solution, and as an artist I want to bring out the oneness of human life.

Hollywood, unfortunately, is preserving and reinforcing the Negro stereotypes. It can't or won't grapple with high seriousness. The Broadway stage is more helpful.

As to his own work—Wright has no set plans. "I'll write whatever my imagination dictates." Now in his middle thirties, he has behind him four books, two of them Book-of-the-Month Club selections—*Black Boy* and *Native Son*. Richard Wright's explosive talent, already widely recognized, is one of tomorrow's brightest promises in American writing.

As an artist Wright can improve on *Black Boy*. The autobiography fails in one crucial respect: it does not explain Richard Wright. The personality it presents is passive, a jumble of emotional tensions and sense impressions.

After meeting Richard Wright one is convinced that he will take a lot of explaining, even with his own pen. Outwardly the author of *Black Boy* is affable, poised, quick to smile, almost gay. When he speaks of the Negro, the tone is intense but still restrained, though the words, written down, are strong stuff. Here perhaps is a clue to this strangely gifted personality. Richard Wright left the South knowing that "I was taking a part of the South to transplant in alien soil," hoping that "it would grow differently, . . . respond to the warmth of other suns, and perhaps bloom." That miracle has happened. But in Richard Wright two forces are still at war, and the North has not yet completely won its battle over the South, which has been so much a part of him.

Part II

♦ ♦ ♦

CONTEMPORARY CRITICAL
RESPONSES

Richard Wright Looks Back

Harsh, Forbidding Memories of Negro Childhood and Youth

W. E. BURGHARDT DU BOIS

◆　◆　◆

T HIS BOOK TELLS A HARSH and forbidding story and
makes one wonder just exactly what its relation to truth is.
The title, "A Record of Childhood and Youth," makes one at first
think that the story is autobiographical. It probably is, at least in
part. But mainly it is probably intended to be fiction or fictionalized biography. At any rate the reader must regard it as creative
writing rather than simply a record of life.

The hero whom Wright draws, and may be it is himself, is in
his childhood a loathsome brat, foul-mouthed and a "drunkard."
The family which he paints is a distressing aggregation. Even toward his mother he never expresses love or affection. Sometimes
he comes almost to sympathy. He wonders why this poor woman,
deserted by her husband, toiling and baffled, broken by paralysis
and disappointment, should suffer as she does. But his wonder is
intellectual inability to explain the suffering. It doesn't seem for
a moment to be personal sorrow at this poor, bowed figure of
pain and ignorance.

The father is painted as gross and bestial, with little of human

Lacking real compassion?

33

sensibility. The grandmother is a religious fanatic, apparently sincere but brutal. The boy fights with his aunt. And here again the artist in Richard Wright seems to fail. He repeats an incident of fighting his aunt with a knife to keep her from beating him. He tells the tale of his grandfather, a disappointed veteran of the Civil War, but tells it without sympathy. The Negroes whom he paints have almost no redeeming qualities. Some work hard, some are sly, some are resentful; but there is none who is ambitious, successful or really intelligent.

After this sordid, shadowy picture we gradually come upon the solution. The hero is interested in himself, is self-centered to the exclusion of everybody and everything else. The suffering of others is put down simply as a measure of his own suffering and resentment. There is scarcely a ray of light in his childhood: he is hungry, he is beaten, he is cold and unsheltered. Above all, a naturally shy and introverted personality is forced back upon itself until he becomes almost pathological. The world is himself and his suffering. He hates and distrusts it. He says, "I was rapidly learning to distrust everything and everybody" [26].

He writes of a mother who wanted him to marry her daughter. "The main value in their lives was simple, clean, good living, and when they thought they had found those same qualities in one of their race they instinctively embraced him, liked him and asked no questions. But such simple unaffected trust flabbergasted me. It was impossible!" [187].

He tells of his own pitiful confusion, when as an imaginative, eager child he could not speak his thought: "I knew how to write as well as any pupil in the classroom, and no doubt I could read better than any of them, and I could talk fluently and expressively when I was sure of myself. Then why did strange faces make me freeze? I sat with my ears and neck burning, hearing the pupils whisper about me, hating myself, hating them" [67].

Then here and there for a moment he forgets his role as artist and becomes commentator and prophet. Born on a plantation, living in Elaine, Arkansas, and the slums of Memphis, he knows the whole Negro race!

After I had outlived the shocks of childhood, after the habit of reflection had been born in me, I used to mull over the strange absence of real kindness in Negroes, how unstable was our tenderness, how lacking in genuine passion we were, how void of great hope, how timid our joy, how bare our traditions, how hollow our memories, how lacking we were in those intangible sentiments that bind man to man, and how shallow was even our despair. [33]

Not only is there this misjudgment of black folk and the difficult repulsive characters among them that he is thrown with, but the same thing takes place with white folk. There is not a single broad-minded, open-hearted white person in his book. One or two start out seemingly willing to be decent, but as he says of one white family for whom he worked, "They cursed each other in an amazingly offhand manner and nobody seemed to mind. As they hurled invectives they barely looked at each other. I was tense each moment, trying to anticipate their wishes and avoid a curse, and I did not suspect that the tension I had begun to feel that morning would lift itself into the passion of my life" [131].

From the world of whites and the world of blacks he grows up curiously segregated. "I knew of no Negroes who read the books I liked, and I wondered if any Negroes ever thought of them. I knew that there were Negro doctors, lawyers, newspaper men, but I never saw any of them" [220].

One rises from the reading of such a book with mixed thoughts. Richard Wright uses vigorous and straightforward English; often there is real beauty in his words even when they are mingled with sadism:

There was the disdain that filled me as I tortured a delicate, blue-pink crawfish that huddled fearfully in the mudsill of a rusty tin can. There was the aching glory in masses of clouds burning gold and purple from an invisible sun. There was the liquid alarm I saw in the blood-red glare of the sun's afterglow mirrored in the squared planes of whitewashed frame houses. There was the languor I felt when I heard green leaves rustling with a rainlike sound. [7]

Yet at the result one is baffled. Evidently if this is an actual record, bad as the world is, such concentrated meanness, filth and despair never completely filled it or any particular part of it. But if the book is meant to be a creative picture and a warning, even then, it misses its possible effectiveness because it is as a work of art so patently and terribly overdrawn.

Nothing that Richard Wright says is in itself unbelievable or impossible; it is the total picture that is not convincing.

Editors' note: Page references to *Black Boy* supplied by the editors in brackets are taken from the 1945 Harper edition.

A Tragic Situation

LIONEL TRILLING

◆　◆　◆

RICHARD WRIGHT's *Black Boy* is a remarkably fine book. Perhaps a Negro's autobiography must always first appear under the aspect of sociology—a fact that is in itself a sociological comment—and *Black Boy* has its importance as a "document," a precise and no doubt largely typical account of Negro life in Mississippi. That it is the account of a tragic situation goes without saying. Here is the Negro poverty in all its sordidness; here is the calculated spiritual imprisonment of one racial group by another; here, above all, is the personal humiliation of Negro by white, the complex cruelty of the dominant race practiced as a kind of personal, spiritual necessity, sometimes direct and brutal, sometimes sophisticated with a sensual, guilty, horrible kindness.

But if *Black Boy* were no more than a document of misery and oppression, it would not have the distinction which in fact it does have. Our literature is full of autobiographical or reportorial or fictional accounts of misery and oppression. I am sure that these books serve a good purpose; yet I find that I feel a little coolness toward the emotions they generate, for it seems to me that too

dangers
of
moral
escape

often they serve the liberal reader as a means of "escape." With honest kinds of "escape" there can be no quarrel—to find a moment's rest in dreams of heroic or erotic fulfillment is as justifiable as sleeping. But the moral "escape" that can be offered by accounts of suffering and injustice is quite another thing. To sit in one's armchair and be harrowed can all too easily pass for a moral or political action. We vicariously suffer in slippers and become virtuous; it is pleasant to exercise moral indignation at small cost; or to fill up emotional vacancy with good strong feeling at a safe distance; or to feel consciously superior to the brutal oppressor; or to be morally entertained by poverty, seeing it as a new and painful kind of primitivism which tenderly fosters virtue or, if not virtue, then at least "reality"; or to indulge in self-pity by projecting it—very pleasant, very flattering, a little corrupting. Mr. Wright's autobiography, so far as it is an account of misery and oppression, does not tempt its readers to such pleasures. This is the mark of the dignity and integrity of the book.

In other words, the sociological aspect of *Black Boy* is the field—I will not say *merely* the field—for a notable exercise of the author's moral and intellectual power. It is difficult to describe that power except, as I have tried to do, by speaking of its effect, by remarking that it does not lead us into easy and inexpensive emotions, although the emotions into which it does lead us are durable. If I try further to understand this, I can only surmise that it comes about because the author does not wholly identify himself with his painful experience, does not, therefore, make himself a mere object of the reader's consciousness, does not make himself that different kind of human being, a "sufferer." He is not an object, he is a subject; he is the same kind of person as his reader, as complex, as free.

Black Boy is an angry book, as it ought to be—we would be surprised and unhappy if it were not. But the amount of anger that Mr. Wright feels is in proportion not only to the social situation he is dealing with; it is also in proportion to the author's desire to live a reasonable and effective life. For what a Negro suffers in the South—what, indeed, he might suffer in the North—calls for illimitable anger. But the full amount of anger that would be appropriate to the social situation alone would surely have the effect of quite destroying the person who felt it. And Mr. Wright, almost from infancy, seems to have refused to be destroyed. For example, by what, as he describes it, seems to have been a kind of blessed unawareness, even a benign stupidity, he simply could not understand the difference between black people and white. That his grandmother was so white as to be almost white may have had something to do with it. In any case, the young Richard had to be taught the difference, and it seems to have been at best a learned thing. This, to be sure, could scarcely have protected him from all psychic wounds and scars. But although he suffered, he seems never to have been passive. He seems thus to have been saved from the terrible ambivalences of the oppressed, from the self-indulgence, the self-pity, the ripe luxuriousness of sensitivity; and he does not, as the oppressed so often do, give himself or his oppressors a false glamour.

Mr. Wright's autobiography does not go beyond the time when he left the South at the age of nineteen. To me this is a disappointment, for Mr. Wright's life after his departure from the South is a great theme—the entrance of an aspiring and relatively ignorant young man into the full stream of national life is always a subject of the richest social and moral interest, and Mr. Wright's race makes that interest the richer. The chapters which appeared in the *Atlantic Monthly* under the title "I Tried to Be a Communist" are not included in *Black Boy;* they are not so interesting as they might be, although they have their point, but they suggest the kind of cultural and social experience I should like to see Mr. Wright explore. He has the directness and honesty to do it well. He has the objectivity which comes from refusing to be an object.

It is this objectivity that allows Mr. Wright to believe that oppression has done something more than merely segregate his people. He dares, that is, to take oppression seriously, to believe that it really does oppress, that its tendency is not so much to exempt the oppressed from the moral flaws of the dominant culture from which they are excluded as it is to give them other flaws of feeling and action. He himself suffered from the fierce puritanical religiosity of his own family. He can speak tenderly of the love that his mother gave him, but he can speak with sorrow and bitterness of the emotional bleakness in which he was reared:

> After I had outlived the shocks of childhood, after the habit of reflection had been born in me, I used to mull over the strange absence of real kindness in Negroes, how unstable was our tenderness, how lacking in genuine passion we were, how void of great hope, how timid our joy, how bare our traditions, how hollow our memories, how lacking we were in those intangible sentiments that bind man to man, and how shallow was even our despair. After I had learned other ways of life I used to brood upon the unconscious irony of those who felt that Negroes led so passional an existence! I saw that what had been taken for our emotional strength was our negative confusions, our flights, our fears, our frenzy under pressure.
>
> Whenever I thought of the essential bleakness of black life in America, I knew that Negroes had never been allowed to catch the full spirit of Western civilization, that they lived somehow in it but not of it. And when I brooded upon the cultural barrenness of black life, I wondered if clean, positive tenderness, love, honor, loyalty, and the capacity to remember were native with man. I asked myself if these human qualities were not fostered, won, struggled and suffered for, preserved in ritual from one generation to another. [33]

I suppose that it is for saying this, or other things of a similar objectivity, that Mr. Wright has, as I have heard, come under the fire of his own people. And that, perhaps, is understandable. But if, like Mr. Wright, we believe that oppression is real, we must sadly praise his courage in seeing that it does not merely affect the body but also the soul. It is only a grim and ironic justice that the deterioration is as great in the oppressor as in the oppressed.

Editor's note: Page reference to *Black Boy* supplied by the editors in brackets is taken from the 1945 Harper edition.

Portrait of a Typical Negro?

MARY MCCARTHY

◆　　◆　　◆

RICHARD WRIGHT's *Black Boy,* a record of his childhood and youth, has provoked a good deal of discussion as to whether he is a "typical" Negro or not. Much of this discussion has been very naive, and probably no white man is in a position to assert, with the positiveness shown by certain conventional reviewers, that the American Negro is not the sullen fury, the secret terrorist, the scoffer, the cynical, disabused spectator of American mores that Wright makes him out to be. On the other hand, no white man, I think, can allow himself to accept Wright's picture as representative, for to do so is to know oneself to be hated, generically, by every Negro in the world.

If the young Richard Wright is typical, then in the kindly servant in the kitchen, the polite red-cap at the Grand Central Station, the serious intellectual at the political meeting, there hides a sardonic Bigger Thomas, watching, condemning, and dreaming voluptuously of murder. But this is intolerable, for though we persist in treating the Negroes as a race (and this is true even of those of us who have Negro friends; it is their color and our emancipated attitude toward it that are the magnetic poles of the relationship), we ourselves wish to be treated by them not as members of a race but as exceptions and individuals— there is hardly an advocate of white supremacy who does not imagine that the inexorable laws of race relations are or ought to be suspended in his particular case, that Negroes steal, lie, cheat, malinger, slack on the job, but certainly not with him; and he will take it as a personal insult, an unforgivable injury to his pride, if his cook, misunderstanding the situation, takes home with her at night a quarter of a pound of butter.

What Richard Wright does in *Black Boy* is to turn the tables on the white reader. Here there are no exceptions; the whites are ethnologically bad—cruel, corrupt, hypocritical, at the very best weak or frightened. Here the white reader is made to feel in his own nerves what it is to be the undifferentiated object of racial animosity. He is not invited, as he is in most works of this kind, to sympathize with the hero, for sympathy is the loophole through which the reader can escape responsibility for the hero's plight and thus become the exception, the "understanding" white man. The reader's experiments at sympathy are met with the harshest rebuffs; the author obdurately, almost perversely, refuses to make himself lovable; he paints himself, and by a deliberate inference, his whole race, as a kind of hardened case of juvenile delinquency. He will not allow himself to be "reached"; he is noncooperative; and the reader is put in the position of an aggrieved social worker whose pious attempts to discover the good in some incorrigible youth are deflected by jeers, obscenities, and vainglorious accounts of his antisocial exploits.

Wright's book tells us, with an uncompromising insistence, that as a boy he was bad and dangerous, feared by his teachers and relations alike. He grew up in poverty, hatred, and hunger. He bit, lied, stole, cut; he killed and tortured animals; at four he was a pyromaniac and at six a drunkard; he was surly, suspicious, brutal, cold, self-pitying; there was no generosity or affection in him. At the end of the book he sets off for Chicago, and if the evidence of this narrative is to be accepted, those who saw him go must have expected him to be traveling on an express highway to the penitentiary or the asylum.

ONE MUST RESPECT WRIGHT for his refusal to give his socially enlightened reader those little luxuries of characterization to which they are accustomed for the intractability that will not allow him to play "the good nigger" even in literature, where no moral ostracism could possibly be incurred for it. Yet, at the same time, there is in his insistence on his own depravity ("I was a drunkard in my sixth year") an element of strain, of self-aggrandizement and self-dramatization that casts a shadow of melodrama on the whole story and permits readers and reviewers to reject the book as "exaggerated" or "distorted." I myself cannot believe in some of the incidents. It is not that I think that Wright invented or edited them for the purpose of this book, but that rather he invented and edited them while they were happening, that he encouraged them, directed them, pushed them this way and that, to conform to a pattern of persecution and revenge, a neurotic pattern of I-and-they, which was already at the age of four the blueprint of his personality.

Long before he became a novelist, the young Richard Wright was making up a story, the story which was his actual life; and to the persons and events of that actual life he behaved as a childish but highly skilled agent provocateur. Of such people it is difficult to say whether their account of experiences is true or false; it is true in the sense that something very like it happened, and false in the sense that it did not happen to the narrator but that on the contrary the narrator happened to it. One feels very strongly throughout the book the pressure of neurotic exploitation. The suffering, hunger, beatings, insults, slights, injuries have had the last drop of pain squeezed out of them by a hand to which the touch of pain is pleasure, so that the suffering qua suffering ceases to exist and we as readers say that we do not believe in it.

FROM ALL THIS WE CANNOT LEAP to the happy conclusion that the sufferings of the Negroes in the South are here grossly exaggerated. They may in fact be underestimated by this writer, whose imagination stood between him and the bleakness and tedium of experience and whose participation in any event was limited by his being, at the same time, the horrified spectator beholding it. The truth is, I think, that *Black Boy* is in a way irrelevant to the situation of the Negro in the South, that the author, who was the victim of a classical Freudian family situation, was already firmly established in the mode of hatred and rejection when he discovered that he was black. His discovery of the Negro question was perhaps for him actually providential, for it furnished a rational ground for the sense of violent estrangement that had been with him since the beginnings of his memory and which, up to the moment of the discovery, must have appeared to him both inexplicable and guilty. Far more than he feared his parents or his relations, this child feared his own nature, the unknown caverns of his personality from which issued rage and murderous impulses that he dared not trace back to their source.

To recognize himself as a Negro was to file himself safely away in the card catalog of the known and the classifiable, to see the rage as socially justified and historically conditioned, to externalize the enemy and the danger. The Negro question, moreover, rescued him from an almost arctic isolation. It humanized his hatred of humanity by converting it into hatred of white society, it inducted him into an army where a minimum of comradeship is inescapable; it substituted the barracks for the cell. Thus the experience of "normal" American society validates the construction of a neurotic; the disease of the system provides a dubious remedy for the sickness of the individual; and this autobiographical fragment is the history of a cure.

The early chapters blur, stammer, tremble with the nervous uncertainty of a speaker who is not sure whether he is telling a lie or not; but as the book moves on, and the crude facts of American life explain and excuse with ever-increasing plausibility the hostility of the Negro boy, it is as though the author himself had become, in the course of living it, convinced of the truth of his story; and as the deprivations, the taunts, the indignities, the provocations that every black man in the South must endure pile on the neck of the victim, he raises his head proudly and his voice, now boldly and justly condemning, grows solemn, loud, and assured.

Richard Wright's Blues

RALPH ELLISON

◆ ◆ ◆

If anybody ask you
who sing this song,
Say it was ole [Black] Boy
done been here and gone.[1]

A S A WRITER, Richard Wright has outlined for himself a
dual role: To discover and depict the meaning of Negro experience, and to reveal to both Negroes and whites those problems of a psychological and emotional nature which arise between
them when they strive for mutual understanding.

Now in *Black Boy*, he has used his own life to probe what
qualities of will, imagination, and intellect are required of a
Southern Negro in order to possess the meaning of his life in the
United States. Wright is an important writer, perhaps the most
articulate Negro American, and what he has to say is highly per-
ceptive. Imagine Bigger Thomas projecting his own life in lucid
prose, guided, say, by the insights of Marx and Freud, and you
have an idea of this autobiography.

Published at a time when any sharply critical approach to Negro life has been dropped as a wartime expendable, it should do
much to redefine the problem of the Negro and American Democracy. Its power can be observed in the shrill manner with
which some professional "friends of the Negro people" have attempted to strangle the work in a noose of newsprint.

What in the tradition of literary autobiography is it like, this
work, described as a "great American autobiography"? As a non-
white intellectual's statement of his relationship to western cul-

ture, *Black Boy* recalls the conflicting pattern of identification and rejection found in Nehru's *Toward Freedom*. In its use of fictional techniques, its concern with criminality (sin) and the artistic sensibility, and in its author's judgment and rejection of the narrow world of his origin, it recalls Joyce's rejection of Dublin in *A Portrait of the Artist*. And as a psychological document of life under oppressive conditions, it recalls *The House of the Dead*, Dostoievski's profound study of the humanity of Russian criminals.

Such works were perhaps Wright's literary guides, aiding him to endow his life's incidents with communicable significance, providing him with ways of seeing, feeling, and describing his environment. These influences, however, were encountered only after these first years of Wright's life were past and were not part of the immediate folk culture into which he was born. In that culture the specific folk-art form which helped shape the writer's attitude toward his life and which embodied the impulse that contributes much to the quality and tone of his autobiography was the Negro Blues. This would bear a word of explanation:

The Blues is an impulse to keep the painful details and episodes of a brutal experience alive in one's aching consciousness, to finger its jagged grain, and to transcend it, not by the consolation of philosophy, but by squeezing from it a near-tragic, near-comic lyricism. As a form, the Blues is an autobiographical chronicle of personal catastrophe expressed lyrically. And certainly Wright's early childhood was crammed with catastrophic incidents. In a few short years his father deserted his mother; he knew intense hunger; he became a drunkard begging drinks from black stevedores in Memphis saloons; he had to flee Arkansas where an uncle was lynched; he was forced to live with a fanatically religious grandmother in an atmosphere of constant bickering; he was lodged in an orphan asylum; he observed the suffering of his mother who became a permanent invalid, while fighting off the blows of the poverty-stricken relatives with whom he had to live; he was cheated, beaten, and kicked off jobs by white employees who disliked his eagerness to learn a trade; and to these objective circumstances must be added the subjective fact that Wright, with his sensitivity, extreme shyness and intelligence was a problem child who rejected his family and was by them rejected.

Thus along with the themes, equivalent descriptions of milieu and the perspectives to be found in Joyce, Nehru, Dostoievski, George Moore and Rousseau, *Black Boy* is filled with blues-tempered echoes of railroad trains, the names of Southern towns and cities, estrangements, fights and flights, deaths and disappointments, charged with physical and spiritual hungers and pain. And like a blues sung by such an artist as Bessie Smith, its lyrical prose evokes the paradoxical, almost surreal image of a black boy singing lustily as he probes his own grievous wound.

In *Black Boy*, two worlds have fused, two cultures merged, two impulses of Western man become coalesced. By discussing some of its cultural sources I hope to answer those critics who would make of the book a miracle and of its author a mystery. And while making no attempt to probe the mystery of the artist (who Hemingway says is "forged in injustice as a sword is forged") I do hold that basically the prerequisites to the writing of *Black Boy* were, on the one hand, the microscopic degree of cultural freedom which Wright found in the South's stony injustice and, on the other, the existence of a personality agitated to a state of almost manic restlessness. There were, of course, other factors, chiefly ideological but these came later.

Wright speaks of his journey north as,

> ... taking a part of the South to transplant in alien soil, to see if it could grow differently, if it could drink of new and cool rains, bend in strange winds, respond to the warmth of other suns, and perhaps, to bloom.... [228]

And just as Wright, the man, represents the blooming of the delinquent child of the autobiography, just so does *Black Boy* represent the flowering—cross-fertilized by pollen blown by the winds of strange cultures—of the humble blues lyric. There is, as in all acts of creation, a world of mystery in this, but there is also enough that is comprehensible for Americans to create the social atmosphere in which other black boys might freely bloom.

For certainly, in the historical sense, Wright is no exception. Born on a Mississippi plantation, he was subjected to all those blasting pressures which, in a scant eighty years, have sent the

Negro people hurtling, without clearly defined trajectory, from slavery to emancipation, from log cabin to city tenement, from the white folks' fields and kitchens to factory assembly lines and which, between two wars, have shattered the wholeness of its folk consciousness into a thousand writhing pieces.

Black Boy describes this process in the personal terms of *one* Negro childhood. Nevertheless, several critics have complained that it does not "explain" Richard Wright. Which, aside from the notion of art involved, serves to remind us that the prevailing mood of American criticism has so thoroughly excluded the Negro that it fails to recognize some of the most basic tenets of western democratic thought when encountering them in a black skin. They forget that human life possesses an innate dignity and mankind an innate sense of nobility; that all men possess the tendency to dream and the compulsion to make their dreams reality; that the need to be ever dissatisfied and the urge ever to seek satisfaction is implicit in the human organism; and that all men are the victims and the beneficiaries of the goading, tormenting, commanding, and informing activity of that imperious process known as the Mind—the Mind, as Valéry describes it, "armed with its inexhaustible questions."

Perhaps all this (in which lies the very essence of the human, and which Wright takes for granted) has been forgotten because the critics recognize neither Negro humanity nor the full extent to which the Southern community renders the fulfillment of human destiny impossible. And while it is true that *Black Boy* presents an almost unrelieved picture of a personality corrupted by brutal environment, it also presents those fresh, human responses brought to its world by the sensitive child:

> There was the *wonder* I felt when I first saw a brace of mountainlike, spotted, black-and-white horses clopping down a dusty road . . . the *delight* I caught in seeing long straight rows of red and green vegetables stretching away in the sun . . . the faint, cool kiss of *sensuality* when dew came on to my cheeks . . . the vague *sense of the infinite* as I looked down upon the yellow, dreaming waters of the Mississippi . . . the echoes of *nos-*

talgia I heard in the crying strings of wild geese ... the *love* I
had for the mute regality of tall, moss-clad oaks ... the hint
of *cosmic cruelty* that I *felt* when I saw the curved timbers of a
wooden shack that had been warped in the summer sun ...
and there was the *quiet terror* that suffused my senses when vast
hazes of gold washed earthward from star-heavy skies on silent
nights. . . . [2] [7–8]

And a bit later, his reactions to religion:

Many of the religious symbols appealed to my sensibilities and
I responded to the dramatic vision of life held by the church,
feeling that to live day by day with death as one's sole thought
was to be so compassionately sensitive toward all life as to view
all men as slowly dying, and the trembling sense of fate that
welled up, sweet and melancholy, from the hymns blended
with the sense of fate that I had already caught from life.
[7–8]

There was also the influence of his mother—so closely linked
to his hysteria and sense of suffering—who (though he only implies it here) taught him, in the words of the dedication prefacing
Native Son, "to revere the fanciful and the imaginative." There were
also those white men—the one who allowed Wright to use his
library privileges and the other who advised him to leave the
South, and still others whose offers of friendship he was too
frightened to accept.

Wright assumed that the nucleus of plastic sensibility is a human heritage—the right and the opportunity to dilate, deepen,
and enrich sensibility—democracy. Thus the drama of *Black Boy*
lies in its depiction of what occurs when Negro sensibility attempts to fulfill itself in the undemocratic South. Here it is not
the individual that is the immediate focus, as in Joyce's *Stephen
Hero*, but that upon which his sensibility was nourished.

Those critics who complain that Wright has omitted the development of his own sensibility hold that the work thus fails as
art. Others, because it presents too little of what they consider

attractive in Negro life, charge that it distorts reality. Both groups miss a very obvious point: That whatever else the environment contained, it had as little chance of prevailing against the overwhelming weight of the child's unpleasant experiences as Beethoven's Quartets would have of destroying the stench of a Nazi prison.

We come, then, to the question of art. The function, the psychology, of artistic selectivity is to eliminate from art form all those elements of experience which contain no compelling significance. Life is as the sea, art a ship in which man conquers life's crushing formlessness, reducing it to a course, a series of swells, tides, and wind currents inscribed on a chart. Though drawn from the world, "the organized significance of art," writes Malraux, "is stronger than all the multiplicity of the world; . . . that significance alone enables man to conquer chaos and to master destiny."

Wright saw his destiny—that combination of forces before which man feels powerless—in terms of a quick and casual violence inflicted upon him by both family and community. His response was likewise violent, and it has been his need to give that violence significance which has shaped his writings.

WHAT WERE THE WAYS by which other Negroes confronted their destiny?

In the South of Wright's childhood there were three general ways: they could accept the role created for them by the whites and perpetually resolve the resulting conflicts through the hope and emotional cartharsis of Negro religion; they could repress their dislike of Jimcrow social relations while striving for a middle way of respectability, becoming—consciously or unconsciously—the accomplices of the whites in oppressing their brothers; or they could reject the situation, adopt a criminal attitude, and carry on an unceasing psychological scrimmage with the whites, which often flared forth into physical violence.

Wright's attitude was nearest the last. Yet, in it there was an all-important qualitative difference: it represented a groping for *individual* values, in a black community whose values were what the young Negro critic, Edward Bland, has defined as "pre-individual." And herein lay the setting for the extreme conflict set off, both within his family and in the community, by Wright's assertion of individuality. The clash was sharpest on the psychological level, for, to quote Bland:

> In the pre-individualistic thinking of the Negro the stress is on the group. Instead of seeing in terms of the individual, the Negro sees in terms of "races," masses of peoples separated from other masses according to color. Hence, an act rarely bears intent against him as a Negro individual. He is singled out not as a person but as a specimen of an ostracized group. He knows that he never exists in his own right but only to the extent that others hope to make the race suffer vicariously through him.

This pre-individual state is induced artificially—like the regression to primitive states noted among cultured inmates of Nazi prisons. The primary technique in its enforcement is to impress the Negro child with the omniscience and omnipotence of the whites to the point that whites appear as ahuman as Jehovah, and as relentless as a Mississippi flood. Socially it is effected through an elaborate scheme of taboos supported by a ruthless physical violence, which strikes not only the offender, but the entire black community. To wander from the paths of behavior laid down for the group is to become the agent of communal disaster.

In such a society the development of individuality depends upon a series of accidents, which often arise, as in Wright's case, from conditions within the Negro family. In Wright's life there was the accident that as a small child he could not distinguish between his fair-skinned grandmother and the white women of the town, thus developing skepticism as to their special status. To this was linked the accident of his having no close contacts with whites until after the child's normal formative period.

But these objective accidents not only link forward to those qualities of rebellion, criminality, and intellectual questioning expressed in Wright's work today. They also link backward into the shadow of infancy where environment and consciousness are so darkly intertwined as to require the skill of a psychoanalyst to define their point of juncture. Nevertheless, at the age of four, Wright set the house afire and was beaten near to death by his frightened mother. This beating, followed soon by his father's desertion of the family, seems to be the initial psychological motivation of his quest for a new identification. While delirious from this beating Wright was haunted "by huge wobbly white bags like the full udders of a cow, suspended from the ceiling above me [and] I was gripped by the fear that they were going to fall and drench me with some horrible liquid" [6].

It was as though the mother's milk had turned acid, and with it the whole pattern of life that had produced the ignorance, cruelty, and fear that had fused with mother-love and exploded in the beating. It is significant that the bags were of the hostile color white, and the female symbol that of the cow, the most stupid (and, to the small child, the most frightening) of domestic animals. Here in dream symbolism is expressed an attitude worthy of an Orestes. And the significance of the crisis is increased by virtue of the historical fact that the lower-class Negro family is matriarchal; the child turns not to the father to compensate if he feels mother-rejection, but to the grandmother, or to an aunt—and Wright rejected both of these. Such rejection leaves the child open to psychological insecurity, distrust, and all of those hostile environmental forces from which the family functions to protect it.

One of the Southern Negro family's methods of protecting the child is the severe beating—a homeopathic dose of the violence generated by black and white relationships. Such beatings as Wright's were administered for the child's own good, a good which the child resisted, thus giving family relationships an undercurrent of fear and hostility, which differs qualitatively from that found in patriarchal middle-class families, because here the severe beating is administered by the mother, leaving the child no parental sanctuary. He must ever embrace violence along with maternal tenderness, or else reject, in his helpless way, the mother.

The division between the Negro parents of Wright's mother's generation, whose sensibilities were often bound by their proximity to the slave experience, and their children, who historically and through the rapidity of American change stand emotionally and psychologically much farther away, is quite deep. Indeed, sometimes as deep as the cultural distance between Yeats's *Autobiographies* and a Bessie Smith blues. This is the historical background to those incidents of family strife in *Black Boy* which have caused reviewers to question Wright's judgment of Negro emotional relationships.

We have here a problem in the sociology of sensibility that is obscured by certain psychological attitudes brought to Negro life by whites.

THE FIRST IS THE ATTITUDE which compels whites to impute to Negroes sentiments, attitudes, and insights which, as a group living under certain definite social conditions, Negroes could not humanly possess. It is the identical mechanism which William Empson identifies in literature as "pastoral." It implies that since Negroes possess the richly human virtues credited to them, then their social position is advantageous and should not be bettered; and, continuing syllogistically, the white individual need feel no guilt over his participation in Negro oppression.

The second attitude is that which leads whites to misjudge Negro passion, looking upon it as they do, out of the turgidity of their own frustrated yearning for emotional warmth, their capacity for sensation having been constricted by the impersonal mechanized relationships typical of bourgeois society. The Negro is idealized into a symbol of sensation, of unhampered social and sexual relationships. And when *Black Boy* questions their illusion they are thwarted much in the manner of the occidental who, after observing the erotic character of a primitive dance, "shacks up" with a native woman—only to discover that far from possessing the hair-trigger sexual responses of a Stork Club "babe," she is relatively phlegmatic.

The point is not that American Negroes are primitives, but that as a group, their social situation does not provide for the type of emotional relationships attributed them. For how could the South, recognized as a major part of the backward third of the nation, flower in the black, most brutalized section of its population, those forms of human relationships achievable only in the most highly developed areas of civilization?

Champions of this "Aren't-Negroes-Wonderful?" school of thinking often bring Paul Robeson and Marian Anderson forward as examples of highly developed sensibility, but actually they are only its *promise*. Both received their development from an extensive personal contact with European culture, free from the influences which shape Southern Negro personality. In the United States, Wright, who is the only Negro literary artist of equal caliber, had to wait years and escape to another environment before discovering the moral and ideological equivalents of his childhood attitudes.

Man cannot express that which does not exist—either in the form of dreams, ideas, or realities—in his environment. Neither his thoughts nor his feelings, his sensibility nor his intellect are fixed, innate qualities. They are processes which arise out of the interpenetration of human instinct with environment, through the process called experience; each changing and being changed by the other. Negroes cannot possess many of the sentiments attributed to them because the same changes in environment which, through experience, enlarge man's intellect (and thus his capacity for still greater change) also modify his feelings; which in turn increase his sensibility, i.e., his sensitivity to refinements of impression and subtleties of emotion. The extent of these changes depends upon the quality of political and cultural freedom in the environment.

Intelligence tests have measured the quick rise in intellect which takes place in Southern Negroes after moving north, but little attention has been paid to the mutations effected in their sensibilities. However, the two go hand in hand. Intellectual complexity is accompanied by emotional complexity; refinement of thought, by refinement of feeling. The movement north affects more than the Negro's wage scale, it affects his entire psychosomatic structure.

The rapidity of Negro intellectual growth in the North is due

partially to objective factors present in the environment, to influences of the industrial city, and to a greater political freedom.
But there are also changes within the "inner world." In the North
energies are released and given *intellectual* channelization—energies
which in most Negroes in the South have been forced to take
either a *physical* form or, as with potentially intellectual types like
Wright, to be expressed as nervous tension, anxiety, and hysteria.
Which is nothing mysterious. The human organism responds to
environmental stimuli by converting them into either physical
and/or intellectual energy. And what is called hysteria is suppressed intellectual energy expressed physically.

The "physical" character of their expression makes for much
of the difficulty in understanding American Negroes. Negro music
and dances are frenziedly erotic; Negro religious ceremonies violently ecstatic; Negro speech strongly rhythmical and weighted
with image and gesture. But there is more in this sensuousness
than the unrestraint and insensitivity found in primitive cultures;
nor is it simply the relatively spontaneous and undifferentiated
responses of a people living in close contact with the soil. For
despite Jimcrow, Negro life does not exist in a vacuum, but in
the seething vortex of those tensions generated by the most
highly industrialized of western nations. The welfare of the most
humble black Mississippi sharecropper is affected less by the flow
of the seasons and the rhythm of natural events than by the
fluctuations of the stock market; even though, as Wright states
of his father, the sharecropper's memories, actions, and emotions
are shaped by his immediate contact with nature and the crude
social relations of the South.

All of this makes the American Negro far different from the
"simple" specimen for which he is taken. And the "physical" quality offered as evidence of his primitive simplicity is actually the
form of his complexity. The American Negro is a western type
whose social condition creates a state which is almost the reverse
of the cataleptic trance: Instead of his consciousness being lucid
to the reality around it while the body is rigid, here it is the body
which is alert, reacting to pressures which the constricting forces
of Jimcrow block off from the transforming, concept-creating ac-

tivity of the brain. The "eroticism" of Negro expression springs from much the same conflict as that displayed in the violent gesturing of a man who attempts to express a complicated concept with a limited vocabulary; thwarted ideational energy is converted into unsatisfactory pantomime, and his words are burdened with meanings they cannot convey. Here lies the source of the basic ambiguity of *Native Son*, whereto in order to translate Bigger's complicated feelings into universal ideas, Wright had to force into Bigger's consciousness concepts and ideas which his intellect could not formulate. Between Wright's skill and knowledge and the potentials of Bigger's mute feelings lay a thousand years of conscious culture.

In the South the sensibilities of both blacks and whites are inhibited by the rigidly defined environment. For the Negro there is relative safety as long as the impulse toward individuality is suppressed. (Lynchings have occurred because Negroes painted their homes.) And it is the task of the Negro family to adjust the child to the Southern milieu; through it the currents, tensions, and impulses generated within the human organism by the flux and flow of events are given their distribution. This also gives the group its distinctive character. Which, because of Negroes' suppressed minority position, is very much in the nature of an elaborate but limited defense mechanism. Its function is dual: to protect the Negro from whirling away from the undifferentiated mass of his people into the unknown, symbolized in its most abstract form by insanity, and most concretely by lynching; and to protect him from those unknown forces *within himself* which might urge him to reach out for that social and human equality which the white South says he cannot have. Rather than throw himself against the charged wires of his prison he annihilates the impulses within him.

The pre-individualistic black community discourages individuality out of self-defense. Having learned through experience that the whole group is punished for the actions of the single member, it has worked out efficient techniques of behavior control. For in many Southern communities everyone knows everyone else and is vulnerable to his opinions. In some communities everyone is

Black culture poses as much of a threat to the individual as white oppression.

"related" regardless of blood-ties. The regard shown by the group for its members, its general communal character, and its cohesion are often mentioned. For by comparison with the coldly impersonal relationships of the urban industrial community, its relationships are personal and warm.

Black Boy, however, illustrates that this personal quality, shaped by outer violence and inner fear, is ambivalent. Personal warmth is accompanied by an equally personal coldness, kindliness by cruelty, regard by malice. And these opposites are as quickly set off against the member who gestures toward individuality as a lynch mob forms at the cry of rape. Negro leaders have often been exasperated by this phenomenon, and Booker T. Washington (who demanded far less of Negro humanity than Richard Wright) described the Negro community as a basket of crabs, wherein should one attempt to climb out, the others immediately pull him back.

The member who breaks away is apt to be more impressed by its negative than by its positive character. He becomes a stranger even to his relatives and he interprets gestures of protection as blows of oppression—from which there is no hiding place, because every area of Negro life is affected. Even parental love is given a qualitative balance akin to "sadism." And the extent of beatings and psychological maimings meted out by Southern Negro parents rivals those described by the nineteenth-century Russian writers as characteristic of peasant life under the czars. The horrible thing is that the cruelty is also an expression of concern, of love.

In discussing the inadequacies for democratic living typical of the education provided Negroes by the South, a Negro educator has coined the term *mis-education*. Within the ambit of the black family this takes the form of training the child away from curiosity and adventure, against reaching out for those activities lying beyond the borders of the black community. And when the child resists, the parent discourages him; first with the formula, "That there's for white folks. Colored can't have it," and finally with a beating.

It is not, then, the family and communal violence described

by *Black Boy* that is unusual, but that Wright *recognized* and made no peace with its essential cruelty—even when, like a babe freshly emerged from the womb, he could not discern where his own personality ended and it began. Ordinarily, both parent and child are protected against this cruelty—seeing it as love and finding subjective sanction for it in the spiritual authority of the Fifth Commandment, and on the secular level in the legal and extra-legal structure of the Jimcrow system. The child who did not rebel, or who was unsuccessful in his rebellion, learned a maso-chistic submissiveness and a denial of the impulse toward western culture when it stirred within him.

WHY THEN HAVE SOUTHERN WHITES, who claim to "know" the Negro missed all this? Simply because they too are armored against the horror and the cruelty. Either they deny the Negro's humanity and feel no cause to measure his actions against civi-lized norms; or they protect themselves from their guilt in the Negro's condition and from their fear that their cooks might poison them, or that their nursemaids might strangle their infant charges, or that their field hands might do them violence, by attributing to them a superhuman capacity for love, kindliness, and forgiveness. Nor does this in any way contradict their stere-otyped conviction that all Negroes (meaning those with whom they have no contact) are given to the most animal behavior.

It is only when the individual, whether white or black, *rejects* the pattern that he awakens to the nightmare of his life. Perhaps much of the South's regressive character springs from the fact that many, jarred by some casual crisis into wakefulness, flee hys-terically into the sleep of violence or the coma of apathy again. For the penalty of wakefulness is to encounter ever more violence and horror than the sensibilities can sustain unless translated into some form of social action. Perhaps the impassioned character so noticeable among those white Southern liberals so active in the Negro's cause is due to their sense of accumulated horror; their passion—like the violence in Faulkner's novels—is evidence of a profound spiritual vomiting.

This compulsion is even more active in Wright and the increasing number of Negroes who have said an irrevocable "no" to the Southern pattern. Wright learned that it is not enough merely to reject the white South, but that he had also to reject that part of the South which lay within. As a rebel he formulated that rejection negatively, because it was the negative face of the Negro community upon which he looked most often as a child. It is this he is contemplating when he writes:

> Whenever I thought of the essential bleakness of black life in America, I knew that Negroes had never been allowed to catch the full spirit of Western civilization, that they lived somehow in it but not of it. And when I brooded upon the cultural barrenness of black life, I wondered if clean, positive tenderness, love, honor, loyalty, and the capacity to remember were native to man. I asked myself if these human qualities were not fostered, won, struggled and suffered for, preserved in ritual from one generation to another. [33]

But far from implying that Negroes have no capacity for culture, as one critic interprets it, this is the strongest affirmation that they have. Wright is pointing out what should be obvious (especially to his Marxist critics) that Negro sensibility is socially and historically conditioned; that western culture must be won, confronted like the animal in a Spanish bullfight, dominated by the red shawl of codified experience, and brought heaving to its knees.

Wright knows perfectly well that Negro life is a by-product of western civilization, and that in it, if only one possesses the humanity and humility to see, are to be discovered all those impulses, tendencies, life and cultural forms, to be found elsewhere in western society.

The problem arises because the special condition of Negroes in the United States, including the defensive character of Negro life itself (the "will toward organization" noted in the western capitalist appears in the Negro as a will to camouflage, to dissimulate) so distorts these forms as to render their recognition as difficult as finding a wounded quail against the brown and yellow leaves of a Mississippi thicket—even the spilled blood blends with the background. Having himself been in the position of the quail— to expand the metaphor—Wright's wounds have told him both the question and the answer which every successful hunter must discover for himself: "Where would I hide if *I* were a wounded quail?" But perhaps that requires more sympathy with one's quarry than most hunters possess. Certainly it requires such a sensitivity to the shifting guises of humanity under pressure as to allow them to identify themselves with the human content, whatever its outer form, and even with those Southern Negroes to whom Paul Robeson's name is only a rolling sound in the fear-charged air.

Let us close with one final word about the Blues: Their attraction lies in this, that they at once express both the agony of life and the possibility of conquering it through sheer toughness of spirit. They fall short of tragedy only in that they provide no solution, offer no scapegoat but the self. Nowhere in America today is there social or political action based upon the solid realities of Negro life depicted in *Black Boy*; perhaps that is why, with its refusal to offer solutions, it is like the Blues. Yet, in it thousands of Negroes will for the first time see their destiny in public print. Freed here of fear and the threat of violence, their lives have at last been organized, scaled down to possessable proportions. And in this lies Wright's most important achievement: He has converted the American Negro impulse toward self-annihilation and "going underground" into a will to confront the world, to evaluate his experience honestly and throw his findings unashamedly into the guilty conscience of America.

Notes

Editors' note: Page references to *Black Boy* supplied by the editors in brackets are from the 1945 Harper edition.

1. Signature formula used by blues singers at conclusion of song.
2. Italics mine.

Part III

♦ ♦ ♦

SCHOLARLY AND CRITICAL
ASSESSMENTS

The Metamorphosis of Richard Wright's
Black Boy

JANICE THADDEUS

◆　◆　◆

THERE ARE TWO KINDS of autobiography—defined and open. In a defined autobiography, the writer presents his life as a finished product. He is likely to have reached a plateau, a moment of resolution which allows him to recollect emotion in tranquillity. This feeling enables him to create a firm setting for his reliable self, to see this self in relief against society or history. Frederick Douglass's *Narrative of the Life of Frederick Douglass*, for instance, is a defined autobiography, a public document, moving undeviatingly from self-denial to self-discovery. It rests on the fulcrum of: "You have seen how a man was made a slave; you shall see how a slave was made a man."[1] The writer of an open autobiography differs from Douglass and others like him in that he is searching, not telling, so that like Boswell or Rousseau he offers questions instead of answers. He does not wish to supply a fulcrum, does not proffer conclusions and solutions, and consequently he refrains from shaping his life neatly in a teleological plot. The tone and purpose of an open autobiography are entirely different from a defined autobiography. Therefore, if an author needs to write an open autobiography, it must not be changed into the defined variety. But Richard Wright's *Black Boy* experienced such a metamorphosis.

The publishing history of *Black Boy* is most fully told in Michel Fabre's afterword to Wright's other autobiographical work, *American Hunger,* which was released in 1977. However, even in Fabre's account, some of the important details are hazy. It is the purpose of this essay to clarify the entire incident and to document the metamorphosis of *Black Boy.*

Wright's *Black Boy,* published in 1945, is—so far as plot goes— molded and shapely, beginning in speechlessness and anger, and ending in articulateness and hope. The boy who at the age of four set fire to his own house, became a drunkard at the age of six, and was so frightened of a new school that he could not write his name on the board, by the final pages has fought and lied his way out of the racist South. The book fits into the familiar plot of the slave narrative. And it ends twenty years before its publication, a long swath of time during which the author has become a famous novelist, writer of *Native Son.* To a degree which has puzzled many readers, however, *Black Boy* also introduces oppositions—both imagistic and thematic—which it never resolves.

Black Boy's epigraph sets its theme, but that theme is paradoxical. Wright initiates his book with an unsettling quotation from Job: "They meet with darkness in the daytime / And they grope at noonday as in the night." Darkness and daytime, black and white, are insistent images throughout. Given the subject matter, this is an obvious choice, but Wright presents his oppositions with puzzling complexity. He mentions in passing in the opening paragraph that his grandmother is white, but it is not until fifty pages later that we discover that Granny was a slave, that she bears the name as well as the color of her white owner, that she does not know—or does not care to know—who her father was. If Granny is white, why is she black? The question is simple, but the answer is not, and Wright emphasizes this indefiniteness. In many scenes, as Gayle Gaskill has shown, Wright deliberately reverses the usual connotations Western tradition has assigned to black and white—that black is always bad and white is good.[2] For instance, when Wright's mother beats him nearly to death for setting their house on fire, he has a feverish dream. "Huge wobbly white bags, like the full udders of cows," hang menacingly over him, and their whiteness is terrifying. Further, although they look like udders and therefore must represent mothers' milk, they threaten to engulf the four-year-old Wright in "some horrible liquid."[3] His mother has become his potential destroyer, and although she is black, her milk is white, and whiteness is evil. In the earlier version of this dream published in *Uncle Tom's Children*, the nightmare is attached to an incident where in a fight with a white gang a flung bottle cuts Wright behind the ear. Here, the apparitions are menacing white faces, a simpler and less psychologically determined image. In *Black Boy*, Wright's mother, like his grandmother, is a mixture of black and white. Although it is true that in *Black Boy* white images are often repressive and black images are often positive, Wright does not entirely deny the traditional meanings of the words. Wright's poodle Betsy is white, and he loves her whiteness, but he will not sell her to white people. If he has to use a blackboard, he emphasizes that the chalk is white. The chalk represents education—and terror. Throughout *Black Boy* Wright's imagery of black and white resists simple formulations. He has not shaped and tailored it to a simple, clear purpose.

The imagery of light and dark is similarly mutable. The South is dark, so dark that Wright frequently wonders over the fact that the sun is still shining. When he hears that an acquaintance has been lynched for presumably consorting with a white prostitute, it seems uncanny that life can continue: "I stood looking down the quiet, sun-filled street. Bob had been caught by the white death" (p. 190). Here, although the light is beautiful, whiteness means death. As readers, we recognize the reference to the black death and are forced to the analogy that the animals carrying this plague are human. When Pease and Reynolds force Wright out of the optical shop where he had hoped to learn a trade, to help people literally to improve their vision, he recounts: "I went into the sunshine and walked home like a blind man" (p. 212). The sun shines, but not for him. In ironic and various ways, then, aesthetically and thematically, the book fulfills its epigraph. The result, however, is anxiety, not resolution.

Black Boy is a violent book, but it has not been sufficiently noted that violence is always linked with its opposite, in a poised opposition resembling the metaphorical tension just discussed. Wright's experiences have made him "strangely tender and cruel, violent and peaceful" (p. 112). Besides the imagery mentioned above, Wright's chief word for this indefinable yearning is hunger. The word and the fact of hunger recur like drumbeats throughout the book, an insistent refrain. Wright never has enough to eat: he steals food even when there is plenty; he receives an orange for Christmas and eats it with preternatural care; he fills his aching stomach with water; he is too thin to pass the postal examination. The hunger is both "bodily and spiritual" (p. 147), and the spiritual hunger is as insistent as its bodily counterpart. The entire book is strung between hunger and satisfaction, as well as light and dark, black and white, and similarly opposing, irreconcilable forces. The word *tension* appears so many times that Wright had to cut out thirty instances of it in the final draft.[4]

Among these oppositions the narrator becomes an immensely powerful but undefined force. Wright himself said, "One of the things that made me write is that I realize that I'm a very average Negro. . . . maybe that's what makes me extraordinary."[5] This recognition of the self as typical is frequent in black autobiography, where beleaguering social forces chain the writer to his race. On the other hand, Wright also said, "I'm merely using a familiar literary form to unload many of the memories that have piled up in me, and now are coming out."[6] These views are quite incompatible, since an average person would not have to unload memories, and their rendering as competing forces in Black Boy is one of its greatest sources of interest—and tension.

But in spite of Black Boy's insistent refusal to resolve the oppositions upon which it rests, the final six pages nonetheless attempt to summarize the preceding experiences, to explain them, give them a defined significance. Wright asks, "From where in this southern darkness had I caught a sense of freedom?" (p. 282). And he proceeds to answer his question. He argues that books alone had kept him "alive in a negatively vital way" (p. 282), especially books by "Dreiser, Masters, Mencken, Anderson, and Lewis," which

> seemed defensively critical of the straitened American environment. These writers seemed to feel that America could be shaped nearer to the hearts of those who lived in it. And it was out of these novels and stories and articles, out of the emotional impact of imaginative constructions of heroic or tragic deeds, that I felt touching my face a tinge of warmth from an unseen light; and in my leaving I was groping toward that invisible light, always trying to keep my face so set and turned that I would not lose the hope of its faint promise, using it as my justification for action. (p. 283)

Jesus tow/a Jerusalem

These final words counteract the paradoxes of the epigraph. The black boy who was heading north was still blind at noonday, but he felt "warmth from an unseen light," and that warmth was hope. He was groping, but groping toward something. The ultimate paragraph states that Wright's search was for the essential significance of life:

> With ever watchful eyes and bearing scars, visible and invisible, I headed North, full of a hazy notion that life could be lived with dignity, that the personalities of others should not be violated, that men should be able to confront other men without fear or shame, and that if men were lucky in their living on earth they might win some redeeming meaning for their having struggled and suffered here beneath the stars. (p. 285)

Even though this last paragraph is presented conditionally, it is strong and eloquent. The promise, even the faint promise, of "redeeming meaning" seems adequate to the dignity of "having struggled and suffered here beneath the stars." We feel that hunger has at last changed to hope.

But this final statement, wrapping up and rounding out the book, is not what Wright had originally planned to publish when he finished *Black Boy* in December 1943. As is now well known, the book was half again as long, and its title was *American Hunger*. It reached page proofs, and its jacket was designed. The full autobiography ends in 1937, ten years later than *Black Boy*, only six years before the actual writing of the book. Therefore, Wright had not achieved the sort of distance from his material which the shortened *Black Boy* implied. Partly for this reason, the full *American Hunger*—as distinct from the published *Black Boy*—retains that tentativeness which is the hallmark of the open autobiography.

In addition, the omitted second section of the autobiography expresses the tensions, the unresolved conflicts, of the first. *American Hunger* is the story, chiefly, of Wright's unsatisfying relationship with the Communist party. Here, the themes of black and white are more subdued, but the theme of hunger persists and becomes more elaborate and universal. Of course, the question of black and white as a simple issue of race continues, but as Wright notes, he now feels "a different sort of tension,"[7] a different kind of "insecurity" (p. 3). The distinction now is likely to be animal and human, dirty and clean. A reconsideration of *Black Boy*'s epigraph will best illustrate the qualities of the omitted section and its relationship to the whole.

The epigraph from Job which prefaced *Black Boy* was originally meant to summarize the entire *American Hunger*. The first line, "They meet with darkness in the daytime," summarizes the action of *Black Boy*. The second line, "And they grope at noonday as in the night," although not denying the content of *Black Boy*, more properly applies to the second section of the book. When Wright first enters a John Reed Club, it seems that neither he nor the members of the club need to grope; they ignore his blackness, and he feels for the first time totally human. But soon they begin to reduce his humanity in other ways. The Communists thwart his attempts to write biographies of their black members:

> I had embraced their aims with the freest impulse I had ever
> known. I, the chary cynic, the man who had felt that no idea
> on earth was worthy of self-sacrifice, had publicly identified

myself with them, and now their suspicion of me hit me with
a terrific impact, froze me within. I groped in the noon sun.
(p. 86)

The isolation Wright feels is different from what he experienced
in the South, but it is in some ways more terrible. He is still
blind, groping even in the sunshine.

Wright had also picked separate epigraphs and titles for each
of the subdivisions of the original *American Hunger*, and when these
are properly replaced, they reassert the anxiety, hunger, and
searching. In its original form, *Black Boy–American Hunger* had specific titles for each book, and each book carried a separate epigraph. *Black Boy* was to be called "Southern Night," and its epigraph was also from Job: "His strength shall be hunger-bitten, /
And destruction shall be ready at his side."[8] The dark imagery of
the "Southern Night" fulfilled its title, as did its violence and
hunger. The second part was to be called "The Horror and the
Glory," and its epigraph came from a Negro folk song:

> Sometimes I wonder, huh,
> Wonder if other people wonder, huh,
> Sometimes I wonder, huh,
> Wonder if other people wonder, huh,
> Just like I do, oh my Lord, just like I do!

This brief verse indicates tentativeness, indecision, and a total lack
of communication. In company with this resistance to conclu-
siveness, Wright emphasizes throughout his sense of wonder, his
innocence: "how wide and innocent were my eyes, as round and
open and dew-wet as morning-glories" (p. 111). Besides elaborat-
ing on its epigraph, the section called "The Horror and the Glory"
explicitly defines its subtitle. In a climactic scene toward the end
of the book, Wright's friend Ross confesses in an open trial that
he has fought the policies of his fellow Communists. The glory
of this moment is that Ross "had shared and accepted the vision
that had crushed him" (p. 124), the vision that all men are equal
and sharing in a communal world. But the horror is that this

vision has been oversimplified by its followers, that they have allowed the party to truncate their abilities to think. Wright says, "This, to me, was a spectacle of glory; and yet, because it had condemned me, because it was blind and ignorant, I felt that it was a spectacle of horror" (p. 125). Wright is a writer, and as such it is his business to search deep into the human heart, to name blindness when he sees it. This is of necessity a lonely search, and a complex one. Like the protagonist of *The Man Who Lived Underground*, on which Wright was working during the years when he was finishing *American Hunger*, a writer may find himself separate from the rest, observing, innocent, condemned.

The final pages of the full *American Hunger*, unlike those of the revised *Black Boy*, do not in fact explain how Wright managed to separate himself from his black confreres in the South, how he became a writer. They do not even hint at his future successes, but rather at his sense of quest, and as Michel Fabre has put it, his feeling that the quest was unfinished and perhaps unfinishable. Wright did not plan to create in his readers nor to accept in himself a feeling of satisfaction, but of hunger, "a sense of the hunger for life that gnaws in us all" (p. 135). Here, too, Wright returns to his imagery of darkness and light: "Perhaps, I thought, out of my tortured feelings I could fling a spark into this darkness" (p. 134). The terminology is similar to Conrad's at the end of *Heart of Darkness*, with reference to the continent before him and its immensity. Wright no longer believes in the Communist vision, no longer yearns for what Fishbelly's father in *The Long Dream* calls "the dream that can't come true,"[9] asserts that he is working "humbly now, with no vaulting dream of achieving a vast unity." Wright knows that his effort is tentative and minimal, but also that he must try to write on the "white paper":

> I would hurl words into this darkness and wait for an echo, and if an echo sounded, no matter how faintly, I would send other words to tell, to march, to fight, to create a sense of the hunger for life that gnaws in us all, to keep alive in our hearts a sense of the inexpressibly human. (p. 135)

This statement is an admission that Wright cannot produce a work that is neat and conclusive, and as a result, the content and effect of these final pages clash with the revised ending of *Black Boy*.

To understand why Wright's conclusion to *Black Boy* is so mismatched with the deliberate inconclusiveness of his full autobiography, one must consider in detail the events surrounding its writing. After the extraordinary success of *Native Son* in 1940, Wright turned to a novel about women, servants, and the problem of those who attempt to pass for white. This novel was never to be finished, but he was working at it consistently until 9 April 1943, when he gave a talk at Fisk University in Nashville. He had not prepared his remarks in advance, and he decided at the last minute to talk about his own life, to be honest with his audience. After the publication of *Black Boy*, he recounted this experience:

> I gave a clumsy, conversational kind of speech to the folks, white and black, reciting what I felt and thought about the world; what I remembered about my life, about being a Negro. There was but little applause. Indeed, the audience was terribly still, and it was not until I was halfway through my speech that it crashed upon me that I was saying things that Negroes were not supposed to say publicly, things that whites had forbidden Negroes to say. What made me realize this was a hysterical, half-repressed, tense kind of laughter that went up now and then from the white and black faces.[10]

This experience convinced him that he ought to finish the book about his own life which he had long been writing in pieces. "The Ethics of Living Jim Crow," for instance, written in 1937, he would eventually transport bodily into his autobiography.[11] The book which he now set out to write, although revised, shaped, and ordered, was primarily an effort to tell the truth, not to convince a particular audience, black or white. Indeed, Wright wrote to his editor at Harper's, Edward Aswell, about a juvenile edition of *Black*

Boy that "I'm just too self-conscious when I write for a special audience."[12] He could not finish the juvenile edition.

The search for truth, for as much truth as one can possibly set down, is the primary motive of a writer of an open as opposed to a defined autobiography. He is not trying primarily to please an audience, to create an aesthetically satisfying whole, but to look into his heart. This attempt is perhaps the most difficult a writer can undertake, requiring as Wright put it in his Fisk speech "real hard terror."

> If you try it, you will find at times sweat will break out upon you. You will find that even if you succeed in discounting the attitudes of others to you and your life, you must wrestle with yourself most of all, fight with yourself; for there will surge up in you a strong desire to alter facts, to dress up your feelings. You'll find that there are many things that you don't want to admit about yourself or others. As your record shapes itself up, an awed wonder haunts you. And yet there is no more exciting an adventure than trying to be honest in this way. The clean, strong feeling that sweeps you when you've done it, makes you know that.... Well, it's quite inexplicable.[13]

When Wright had at last, through a multitude of drafts, faced and finished these truths and these terrors, he forwarded his manuscript to his agent, Paul Reynolds. Reynolds sent the manuscript, which was at that moment called "Black Hunger," to Harper's, where Aswell was expecting the novel about the problems of attempting to "pass." Aswell instantly recognized the autobiography's worth, however, and within three days had sent an advance. By this time the title was "American Hunger." The unsigned reader's notes (presumably Aswell's) preserved in the Harper papers suggest, among other things, that Wright cut out some of the John Reed section. The reader adds, "I may be wrong but I personally would like to see some of this cut and the story carried on to the years of Wright's success—perhaps to the writing of *Native Son*. His own feeling of hope, his own preservation through adversity would somehow be justified as it is not here."[14] It is an editor's business to ask that even lives be given justification, that order be imposed, that readers be given a sense of wholeness and completion. The suggestion that the autobiography be brought up to *Native Son* was somehow dropped, but Wright cut the John Reed section as much as he could. He rewrote the ending, but it resisted closure: "I tried and tried to strengthen the ending. One thing is certain, I cannot step outside of the mood rendered there and say anything without its sounding false. So, what I've done is this: I've expanded the end to deepen the mood, to hint at some kind of emotional resolution."[15] The book moved toward its final stages. Wright objected to the phrase "courageous Negro" in the jacket copy and asked that it be changed to "Negro American," which "keeps the book related to the American scene and emphasizes the oneness of impulse, the singleness of aim of both black and white Americans."[16] Wright's emphasis, once again, is on a general audience. He is trying to tell the truth, avoiding the need to mask, modify, change, which had characterized his life in white America. He is deviating from the model of the black slave narrative, which moved teleologically from slavery into freedom, from dehumanization to fulfillment. The pressure to round out the book was strong, but Wright successfully resisted.

The further metamorphosis, the addition of the final six pages to *Black Boy*, took place in the spring of 1944, after *American Hunger* in its entirety had been forwarded to the Book-of-the-Month Club. There, the judges said that they would accept the book on condition that the second section be cut off and the first section be provided with more complete resolution. On 26 June, Aswell forwarded a draft of the new conclusion in which Wright had "tried to carry out a suggestion made by Mr. Fadiman to the effect that he summarize briefly, and make explicit, the meaning that is now implicit in the preceding pages."[17]

Dorothy Canfield Fisher, who had written the introduction for *Native Son*, urged Wright to expand somewhat on his first draft and to seek out the American sources for his feelings of hope:

> From what other source than from the basic tradition of our
> country could the soul of an American have been filled with
> that "hazy notion" that life could be lived with dignity? Could
> it be that even from inside the prison of injustice, through the
> barred windows of that Bastille of racial oppression, Richard
> Wright had caught a glimpse of the American flag?[18]

With America at war, this spirit of patriotism was the general
mood, and elsewhere Fisher contrasts American freedom with
Nazi repression. Reflecting similar fervor, Aswell's list of possible
titles for the truncated first half of *American Hunger* includes, besides fifteen evocations of darkness such as "Raw Hunger" and
"The Valley of Fear," these familiar complacencies: "Land of the
Free" and "Land of Liberty."[19] Wright replied that the Negro environment was such that very few could intuit the American
way. Even these could desire nothing specific; they could feel
only a hope, a hunger. He emphasized that accident, not fate or
choice, had more often than not governed his own life. However, Fisher had suggested that Wright consider which American
books might have influenced him, given him a vision of America
which had inspired him. In response to this request, Wright
added two more paragraphs. One defined his hope—or more
precisely refused to define his hope, showing that he was simply
running away from violence and darkness, not toward anything
he could formulate. The second paragraph had to do with his
reading. Although Wright was careful to emphasize that his
reading had been accidental, that the books were alien, that
Dreiser, Masters, Mencken, Anderson, and Lewis were critical of
the American environment, he did give his hope a nearer reality.
Even so, as mentioned above, he called it "a warmth from an
unseen light," a phrase which Fisher praised with special emphasis. Wright had actually transported this phrase from *American
Hunger*, where it appeared in a much more nebulous context:
"Even so, I floundered, staggered; but somehow I always groped
my way back to that path where I felt a tinge of warmth from
an unseen light" (p. 25). Here there is blindness, the groping of

the epigraph, and a tiny waft of hope. The *Black Boy* context, too, mentions groping, but the rhetoric is more assured, the feeling more triumphant.

Indeed, Wright realized that *American Hunger* was no longer an appropriate title for this transformed autobiography. The Book-of-the-Month Club suggested "The First Chapter," which would have emphasized the initiation theme and implied a sequel, but this choice seemed jejune. Wright himself eventually suggested *Black Boy*, and his accompanying comment emphasizes the unity he had attained by truncating his book:

> Now, this is not very original, but I think it covers the book. It is honest. Straight. And many people say it to themselves when they see a Negro and wonder how he lives . . . *Black Boy* seems to me to be not only a title, but also a kind of heading of the whole general theme.[20]

His suggested subtitles, however, retained the sense of process. Nearly all of them contained the word "anxiety." Eventually, however, the subtitle too reflected the pose of completeness. *Black Boy* became "A Record of Childhood and Youth."

No one will ever know how the original *American Hunger* would have fared after publication, but *Black Boy* became an instant bestseller. In 1945 it ranked fourth among nonfiction sales.[21] The content was new and shocking, but even so, many readers noted the hopeful ending. Responses ranged from outrage through misunderstanding and biased readings to unalleviated praise. Senator [Theodore] Bilbo attacked the book from the Right, and Ben Burns hacked away at it from the Left. Black opinion was divided over Wright's frequently sharp comments about members of his own race. Orville Prescott recognized and disliked some of the elements of open autobiography and downgraded the book for its inclusiveness, criticizing Wright's "excessive determination to omit nothing, to emphasize mere filth." Although we have seen that this inclusiveness was a deliberate and necessary choice, Prescott decided that it sprang "from a lack of artistic discrimination and selectivity."[22] Milton Mayer made a similar criticism, defining the book's genre as "history."[23] Lewis Gannett, claiming that "*Black Boy* may be one of the great American autobiographies," saw a double America in the book much like Dorothy Canfield Fisher's: "This, too is America: both the mud and scum in which Richard Wright grew up, and the something that sang within him, that ever since has been singing with an ever clearer, painfully sweeter, voice."[24] Many others used Wright's subsequent career as a defining measure, seeing in his earlier experiences the seeds of his genius. One typical re- view ended: "Soon after this discovery of the great world of books, we find our black boy born of the Mississippi plantation, now nineteen, packing up his bags for new worlds and horizons in the North. The rest of the story is well-known."[25] Readers of *Black Boy*, no matter what their race or persuasion, often made the easy leap from the trip north to bestsellerdom and success.

But for Wright himself this leap was not easy, as readers of *American Hunger* know. Although pieces of the end of the orig- inal *American Hunger* were published in the *Atlantic Monthly* and *Ma- demoiselle* before *Black Boy* itself actually appeared, it obviously could not reach as large an audience as *Black Boy* itself. Constance Webb produced a photo-offset version of the whole manuscript, but this was only privately circulated.[26] Even readers who later read most of this material in *The God That Failed* or in *Eight Men*[27] could not intuit the negative strength of the omitted pages which immediately followed Wright's escape to the North in *American Hunger*. Nothing short of Wright's opening words can convey the desolation he felt on arriving in his hoped-for para- dise: "My first glimpse of the flat black stretches of Chicago depressed and dismayed me, mocked all my fantasies" (p. 1). Wright did at last find a place where he was comfortable, but it was not Chicago or any other place in the United States. In spite of Mencken, Anderson, Dreiser, Masters, and Lewis, the Ameri- can dream which Wright could not honestly elicit in the last pages of his *Black Boy* simply did not exist for him. When Wright arrived in Paris on 15 May 1946, he wrote to his editor at Harper's:

Ed, Paris is all I ever hoped to think it was, with a clear sky, buildings so beautiful with age that one wonders how they happen to be, and with people so assured and friendly and confident that one knows that it took many centuries of living to give them such poise. There is such an absence of race hate that it seems a little unreal. Above all, Paris strikes me as being truly a gentle city, with gentle manners.[28]

Here he could live and work as a human being, released from the ungentleness he could never escape in the United States.

In spite of the tentativeness of Wright's ending for *Black Boy*, in spite of his ultimate emigration, subsequent readers have continued to misread those final pages. Arthur P. Davis, for instance, in *From the Dark Tower* says, "The book ends . . . on a note of triumph. Near the close of the work Wright describes his moment of truth."[29] But there was no moment of truth. Similarly, although Stephen Butterfield describes black autobiography in general as reflecting "a kind of cultural schizophrenia, where the author must somehow discover roots in a country which does not accept him as a human being,"[30] he defines *Black Boy* as one of the modern survivals of the pattern of the slave narrative. In support of this argument, he writes, "The slave narrative's basic pattern, it will be remembered, was an escape from South to North as well as a movement up the social scale from the status of slave to that of respected, educated citizen and vanguard of black politics and culture" (pp. 130–31). Without the *American Hunger* ending, *Black Boy* is indeed modeled on the slave-narrative pattern, but Wright intended the ending to remain ambiguous, groping, hungry. Unfortunately the pattern absorbs the deviating elements, and only an unusually careful reader will notice the hesitancy in the final pages, the conditional verbs, the halting rhetoric, the mention of luck.

In 1977, seventeen years after Wright's death, Harper and Row published *American Hunger* as a separate volume, with an afterword by Michel Fabre giving a brief outline of its publishing history. Fabre objected to the disjoining of the two parts of the original autobiography, observing, "*Black Boy* is commonly construed as a typical success story, and thus it has been used by the American liberal to justify his own optimism regarding his country" (p. 140). The rhetoric is strong, but the point is valid, and indeed it is more generally true than Fabre implies. Davis and Butterfield also misread *Black Boy*, and they cannot easily be grouped with "American liberals." Reviewers of the 1977 *American Hunger*, those of both races and all political persuasions, generally agreed that reading it changes one's perceptions of *Black Boy*. Alden Whitman went one step further, arguing that *American Hunger* did not make sense alone and suggesting: "It would have been more useful, in my opinion, to have issued *Black Boy* complete at last, so that the reader could get the full flavor of the autobiography as Wright initially wrote it."[31]

Many books, through the influence of an editor, have been drastically changed before publication, and the published work is accepted as definitive. What we read is *The Waste Land*, not "He Do the Police in Three Voices." It is true that Wright concurred entirely in the division of *American Hunger* into *Black Boy* and its sequel, even supplying the new title. But, as I have tried to show here, the change was more drastic than Wright meant it to be; the ultimate significance of the book shifted further than Wright had intended. *Black Boy* became a more definitive statement than its themes of hope and hunger could support Therefore, *American Hunger* needs to be reissued in its entirety, with the final six pages of the present *Black Boy* given as an appendix. Failing this, every reader of *Black Boy* should buy both books and read them together, recognizing that the last six pages of *Black Boy* were added in a final revision in part as a response to wartime patriotism. When combined, both of these books emphasize the lack of conviction, the isolation, and finally the lack of order in Wright's world as he saw it, a sadness and disarray which his truncated autobiography *Black Boy*, as published, seems at the end to deny.

Notes

1. *Narrative of the Life of Frederick Douglass, an American Slave, Written by Himself* (1845; reprint, New York: New American Library, 1968), p. 77.

Wherever clear, subsequent citations of works already cited will appear in parentheses in the text.

2. "The Effect of Black/White Imagery in Richard Wright's *Black Boy*," *Negro American Literature Forum* 7 (1973): 46–48.

3. Richard Wright, *Black Boy* (1945; reprint, New York: Harper, 1966), p. 13.

4. Firestone Library, Princeton University, Harper Papers, box 33, folder 17, TS Letter to Edward Aswell, 14 January 1944; these thirty instances were spread over the whole book, including the section now known as *American Hunger*. Materials from the Harper Papers are published with permission from Princeton University Library, Harper and Row Publishers, and Paul Reynolds, Inc.

5. Michel Fabre, *The Unfinished Quest of Richard Wright* (New York: Morrow, 1973), p. 251.

6. Richard Wright, quoted in an interview with JKS, "A Searing Picture of Childhood in the South," *Minneapolis Tribune*, 4 March 1945; reprinted in *Richard Wright: The Critical Reception*, ed. John M. Reilly (New York: Burt Franklin, 1978), p. 131.

7. Richard Wright, *American Hunger* (1977; reprint, New York: Harper, 1983), p. 2.

8. There are many extant copies of the galleys of the original *American Hunger*. I have used the copy in the Richard Wright Archive Collection of American Literature, Beinecke Rare Book and Manuscript Library, Yale University. This copy of the author's proofs, JWJ Wright 20, dated 25–26 April 1944, is complete except for the last page.

9. Garden City, N.Y.: Doubleday, 1958, p. 79.

10. "Richard Wright Describes the Birth of *Black Boy*," *New York Post*, 30 November 1944, p. B6.

11. Fabre, *Quest*, pp. 250–51.

12. Harper Papers, TS, folder 20, 27 November 1944.

13. "Richard Wright Describes the Birth of *Black Boy*."

14. Harper Papers, TS, folder 15.

15. TS Letter to Aswell, 14 January 1944, Harper Papers, folder 17.

16. TS Letter to Aswell, 22 January 1944, Harper Papers, folder 17.

17. TS Letter to Meredith Wood, Harper Papers, folder 18.

18. TS carbon enclosure, 1 July 1944, Harper Papers, folder 18.

19. Harper Papers, folder 19. Wright's replying letter is not available to the general public, but a draft of a response can be found in Beinecke, JWJ, Wright 10.

20. TS Letter to Aswell, 10 August 1944, Harper Papers, folder 19; Fabre, *Quest*, p. 254.

21. Fabre, *Quest*, p. 282.

22. Review in *New York Times*, 28 February 1945, p. 21; reprinted in *Reception*, ed. Reilly, p. 121.

23. "Richard Wright: Unbreakable Negro," *Progressive* 9 (9 April 1945); reprinted in *Reception*, ed. Reilly, p. 154.

24. Review in *New York Herald Tribune*, 28 February 1945, p. 17; reprinted in *Reception*, ed. Reilly, p. 120.

25. James W. Ivy, "*American Hunger*," *Crisis* 52 (1945): 118; reprinted in *Reception*, ed. Reilly, p. 159.

26. Fabre, *Quest*, p. 628.

27. *The God That Failed*, ed. Richard Crossman (New York: Harper, 1949); *Eight Men*, ed. Michel Fabre (Cleveland, Ohio: World, 1961). In the Fabre version of "The Man Who Went to Chicago," the many parentheses are removed, an undoubted improvement which should be transferred to subsequent editions of *American Hunger*.

28. TS, 15 May 1946, Harper Papers, folder 27.

29. *From the Dark Tower: Afro-American Writers, 1900–1960* (Washington, D.C.: Howard University Press, 1974), p. 157.

30. *Black Autobiography in America* (Amherst: University of Massachusetts Press, 1974), p. 94.

31. Review in *Chicago Tribune Book World*, 22 May 1977, sec. 7, p. 1; reprinted in *Reception*, ed. Reilly, p. 376.

From Experience to Eloquence

Richard Wright's Black Boy *as Art*

CHARLES T. DAVIS

◆　◆　◆

N*ATIVE SON*[1] is the work for which Richard Wright is best
known, but *Black Boy*,[2] an autobiography more or less, may
be the achievement that offers the best demonstration of his art
as a writer. This idea is not so startling given Wright's special
talents—the eye of a skilled reporter, the sensibility of a revolutionary poet, alert to varied forms of injustice, and the sense of
symbolic meaning carried by the rituals of ordinary life. The problem up to the present time is not the lack of attention the work
has received. Like *Native Son*, *Black Boy* was selected by the Book-
of-the-Month Club and was thus assured a wide distribution and
a serious if somewhat skewed reading from many critics. In 1970
Stanley Hyman, in reviewing Wright's entire career, assigned *Black
Boy* to a period in which Wright's "important writing" occurred—
according to his definition, Wright's last years as a resident in
America, from 1940 to 1945.[3] But *Black Boy* by itself failed to acquire
as an original work of art the reputation it deserves.

It appears now, from the perspective of a generation, that a
measure of distortion was unavoidable, given the political temper

of the time. The history of the publication of the manuscript entitled *American Hunger*,[4] of which *Black Boy* was a part, encouraged a violent political response. It was well known that "I Tried to Be a Communist," which appeared in the August and September issues of the *Atlantic Monthly* in 1944,[5] were chapters of an autobiographical record to be published the following year, even though they were excluded finally with the rest of the matter dealing with the years in Chicago and New York. When *Black Boy* did appear, knowing critics read the book in light of the much-publicized account of Wright's difficulties with the Communist party. Baldly put, the situation for the critic encouraged a form of outside intrusion, a case of knowing too much, of supplying a frame of reference which a reading of the basic text does not support. The board of the Book-of-the-Month Club or Edward Aswell or both,[6] in suggesting a restriction of the autobiographical matter to the period before migration to Chicago, exercised a judgment that displayed something more than the good sense of successful editors; indeed, that judgment pointed up the artistic integrity of the work. Someone concluded accurately that the intensity of *Black Boy* came from a concentration upon one metaphor of oppression, the South, and prevented the diffusion of power that would be the consequence of the introduction of a second, the Communist party.

If the political reaction created one kind of distortion in the eye of the examiner, more normal literary expectations created another. *Black Boy* baffled W. E. B. Du Bois, the most impressive black intellectual of his time. His review in the New York *Herald Tribune* states his dilemma: "if the book is meant to be a creative picture and a warning, even then, it misses its possible effectiveness because it is as a work of art so patently and terribly overdrawn."[7] By 1945 Du Bois had published three major works with outstanding autobiographical elements, one of which, *Dusk of Dawn*, was a fully developed autobiography of considerable intellectual distinction,[8] and he could not be accused of responding merely to a sense of affront to his middle-class sensibilities. Du Bois was not prepared to accept Wright's bleak Mississippi; he was appalled not so much by the condition of terror there as by a state of mind that denied the possibility of humanity for blacks and frustrated all black efforts to achieve satisfaction beyond the minimal requirements for life. After all, Du Bois had vivid memories of his experience as a young teacher in rural Tennessee, where he encountered aspiring, sensitive pupils who, though often defeated or betrayed by their environment, were not totally crushed by southern oppression.[9] Moreover, Du Bois joined, no doubt, a group of critics of *Black Boy* best defined by Ralph Ellison as consisting of readers who complained that Wright had "omitted the development of his own sensibility."[10] But this is to define sensibility in a way generally understood by the nineteenth century, which is to hold that sensibility is an orderly accretion of the mind and heart within an environment recognizably human, and not to accept Wright's radical equation of the existence of sensibility with survival.

Du Bois did not doubt that autobiography could be art, though more naive critics might. He could not accept the principles of an art as austere as Wright's was, one in which many of the facts of southern life, so familiar to him, were excluded and in which generalization had been carried to such extreme lengths. After all, the book's title was *Black Boy*, not "A Black Boy,"[11] with an appropriately limiting modifier. Viewed superficially, Richard's odyssey was unique primarily because it had a happy ending—the escape from the hell of the South, where, apparently, all of his black associates (he had no friends in the narrative) were destined to spend the rest of their days. Wright's generalizations about the dehumanizing relationships between whites and blacks and the almost equally unsatisfying connections between blacks and blacks shaped his South, and these assumptions Du Bois thought to be distorted. One sweeping statement by young Wright in Memphis, where he lived from his seventeenth to his nineteenth year and where he committed himself formally to becoming a writer,[12] would certainly extract from Du Bois an expression of disbelief, if not annoyance: "I knew of no Negroes who read the books I liked and I wondered if any Negroes ever thought of them. I knew that there were Negro doctors, lawyers, newspapermen, but I never saw any of them. When I read a Negro newspaper I never caught the faintest echo of my preoccupation in its pages."[13]

Not only Du Bois, but also other blacks, even those lacking the knowledge of black life in America which Du Bois had acquired from his surveys and research projects at Atlanta University,[14] would be appalled at Richard's confession of his cultural isolation. This is a moment when generalization approaches fiction, when we must say that a statement may be acceptable within its context, but that it is questionable as a fact standing on its own, as something that might be supported by the confessions of other black boys, especially those emerging from families with middle-class aspirations and pretensions like Wright's.

Editing the raw matter of life is necessary, of course, to write an autobiography with any claim to art. No one has described this activity better than Ellison has in his critical examination of *Black Boy*: "The function, the psychology, of artistic selectivity is to eliminate from an art form all those elements of experience which contain no compelling significance. Life is as the sea, art a ship in which man conquers life's crushing formlessness."[15] What Ellison did not say is that such editing requires the use of controlling principles that are invariably fictional. This is to say that the organizing ideas are assumptions that are not strictly true according to the most objective criteria. Operating from a strict conception of the truth, we have every right to question the emotional basis for *The Education of Henry Adams*, an especially intense form of self-pity coming from the most widely cultivated American of his time, who, nonetheless, constantly reminds us of his lack of preparation for the nineteenth century, not to mention the twentieth. And in *Black Boy* we are asked to accept Richard's cultural isolation as well as his vulnerability to all forms of deprivation—physical, emotional, social, and intellectual.

Some critics, carried off by the impact of *Black Boy*, tend to treat the autobiography as if it were fiction. They are influenced by the fact that much great modern fiction, Joyce's *Portrait of the Artist as a Young Man*, for example, is very close to life. And the tendency here is reinforced by the fact that the author himself, Wright, is a creator of fictions. Yielding so is a mistake because many of the incidents in *Black Boy* retain the sharp angularity of life, rather than fitting into the dramatic or symbolic patterns of fiction. Richard's setting fire to the "fluffy white curtains" (p. 4), and incidentally the house, is not the announcement of the birth of a pyromaniac or a revolutionary, but testimony primarily to the ingenuity of a small black boy in overcoming mundane tedium. We must say "primarily" because this irresponsible act suggests the profound distress and confusion an older Richard would bring to a family that relied heavily upon rigid attitudes toward religion, expected behavior, and an appropriate adjustment to southern life. Richard's fire is not Bigger's rat at the beginning of *Native Son*, when the act of killing brings out pent-up violence in the young black man and foreshadows, perhaps, the events of book two, "Flight," when Bigger's position becomes that of the cornered rat.[16] Nor does Richard's immodest invitation to his grandmother during his bath (p. 49) offer disturbing witness to the emergence of a pornographer or a connoisseur of the erotic; rather, it points to something more general, the singular perversity in Richard that makes him resist family and the South. In *Black Boy* we exist in a world of limited probability that is not life exactly, because there is an order to be demonstrated, and it does not display the perfect design of a serious fiction. We occupy a gray area in between. The patterns are here on several levels. Though they may not be so clear and tight as to permit the critic to predict, they do govern the selection of materials, the rendering of special emphases, distortions, and the style.

We seldom raise questions about what is omitted from an autobiography, yet if we wish to discover patterns, we must begin with what we do not find. The seasonal metaphor in *Walden* (we move from spring to spring) becomes all the more important once we realize that Henry Thoreau lived on the shore of Walden Pond more than two years.[17] Franklin's few "errata"[18] point up the strong aridity of an autobiography that touches so little on the traumas of the heart. Franklin's education, his achievements in business and science, and his proposals for the benefit of society seem at times supported by an emotional substructure far too frail. But the purposes of both autobiographies—in *Walden*, to offer the model of a renewed life; in the *Autobiography of Benjamin Franklin*, to sketch a convincing design of a successful life in the New World, one that emphasizes the practical values that most Americans admired and many Europeans envied—were achieved in part because of the shrewdness in excluding truthful, though extraneous matter. So, too, *Black Boy* profits from rigorous and inspired editing.

One function of the omissions is to strengthen the impression in our minds of Richard's intense isolation. This is no mean achievement given the fact that Wright was born into a large family (on his mother's side, at least) which, despite differences in personality, cooperated in times of need. The father, because of his desertion of his mother, was early in Richard's mind, perhaps in the sentiments of other family members, too, an object of hate and scorn. There are no names in the early pages of *Black Boy*, not even that of Richard's brother, Leon Allan, just a little more than two years younger than Richard. When the names begin to appear in *Black Boy*, they tend to define the objects of adversarial, often violently hostile relationships—Grandmother Wilson, Aunt Addie, Uncle Thomas. Two notable exceptions are Grandfather Wilson, an ineffectual man capable only of reliving his past as a soldier in the Civil War, and Richard's mother, Ella, a pathetically vulnerable woman of some original strength who, because of continuing illness, slipped gradually into a state of helplessness that became for Richard symbolic of his whole life as a black boy in the South.[19]

The admirable biography of Wright by Michel Fabre suggests another dimension for Richard's opponents in his embattled household. The climax of the violence in the family occurred with the confrontation with Uncle Tom, portrayed as a retired and defeated schoolteacher reduced at the time to earning a living by performing odd jobs as a carpenter. Richard resented the fact that he was the victim of Uncle Tom's frustrations, and he responded to orders from the older man by threatening him with razors in both hands and by spitting out hysterically, "You are not an example to me; you could never be. . . . You're a *warning*. Your life isn't so hot that you can tell me what to do. . . . Do you think that I want to grow up and weave the bottoms of chairs for people to sit in?" (p. 140). A footnote from Fabre adds more information about the humiliated uncle:

> The portrait of Uncle Thomas in *Black Boy* is exaggerated. After living with the Wilsons, he moved next door and became a real-estate broker. In 1938, he was a member of the Executive Committee of the Citizen's Civic League in Jackson and wrote a book on the word *Negro*, discussing the superiority complex of the Whites and its effects on the Blacks. At this time Richard put him in contact with Doubleday publishers and the uncle and the nephew were completely reconciled.[20]

Wright includes in *Black Boy* a touching description of meeting his father again after a quarter century. As the newly successful author looked at a strange black sharecropper in ragged overalls holding a muddy hoe, the old resentment for past neglect faded: "I forgave him and pitied him as my eyes looked past him to the unpainted wooden shack" (p. 30). But *Black Boy* contains no softening reconsiderations of Uncle Tom, or of Aunt Addie, who, like her brother, seems to have possessed some redeeming qualities,[21] or of Granny Wilson for that matter. Their stark portraits dominate the family and define a living space too narrow, too mean, and too filled with frustration and poverty for an imaginative youngster like Richard.

A growing boy, when denied the satisfactions of a loving home, looks for emotional support at school or at play, and if he is lucky, he finds something that moderates domestic discontent. But there is little compensation of this sort in *Black Boy*. The reality of the life away from the family seems to be less bleak than Wright represents it, though his schooling was retarded by early irregularity because of the family's frequent moves, and his play restricted, perhaps because of the family's desperate need for money and Granny's Seventh Day Adventist scruples. Once again we are struck by the absence of names—of teachers like Lucy McCranie and Alice Burnett, who taught Richard at the Jim Hill School in Jackson and recognized his lively intelligence,[22] or Mary

L. Morrison or the Reverend Otto B. Cobbins, Richard's instructors in the eighth and ninth grades of the Smith-Robinson School,[23] to whose dedication and competence, despite personal limitations, Wright paid tribute elsewhere.[24] There was no question about his marginal status in these institutions, since Richard stood regularly at the head of his class.

Black Boy is singularly devoid of references to rewarding peer associations. There is no mention of Dick Jordan, Joe Brown, Perry Booker, or Essie Lee Ward, friends of this period and so valued that Wright was in touch with several of them ten years later when he was living in Chicago.[25] The fact that a few of Wright's childhood associates did succeed in making their way to Chicago has an amount of interest in itself, serving as well to break the isolation that Wright has fabricated so well. Among the childhood activities that went unrecorded were the exploits of the Dick Wright clan, made up of a group of neighborhood boys who honored in the name of their society, no doubt, their most imaginative member. The clan included Dick Jordan, Perry Booker, Joe Brown, and also Frank Sims, a descendant of a black senator during the Reconstruction period, Blanche K. Bruce.[26] What is amply clear, then, is that Wright had a childhood more than a little touched by the usual rituals and preoccupations of middle-class boys growing up in America, but what is also apparent is that reference to them would modify our sense of Richard's deprived and disturbed emotional life, a necessity for the art of the autobiography, rather more important than any concern for absolute accuracy.

Wright has little to say directly about sex. Richard's most serious temptation for sexual adventure comes toward the end of *Black Boy* in Memphis, when he is taken in by the Moss family. Richard succeeds in resisting the opportunity to take advantage of a cozy arrangement with Bess, the daughter whom Mrs. Moss seeks to thrust upon him, with marriage as her ultimate objective (p. 185). There are some indirect references to frustrated, sublimated, or distorted forms of sexual energy—in Miss Simon, certainly, the tall, gaunt, mulatto woman who ran the orphan home where Richard was deposited for a period (pp. 25–28). And there were exposures to white women, all calculated to teach Richard the strength of the taboo prohibiting the thought (not to mention the fact) of black-white sexual relations in the South. But Richard never takes an aggressive interest in sex; the adventures that he stumbles into create traumas when they are serious and unavoidable, or are embarrassing when he can resist participation and control his reactions. Wright, indeed, seems to be even more discreet than Franklin was; by comparison, Claude Brown is a raving sensualist in *Manchild in the Promised Land*, though roughly the same period of growth is involved. It is strange that so little space is given to sexual episodes and fantasies in the record of the gradual maturing of an adolescent—unbelievable, given the preoccupations of the twentieth century. We face the problem of omission again. Wright deliberately seeks to deprive his hero, his younger self, of any substantial basis for sensual gratification located outside his developing imagination. The world that *Black Boy* presents is uniformly bleak, always ascetic, and potentially violent, and the posture of the isolated hero, cut off from family, peer, or community support, is rigidly defiant, without the softening effects of interludes of sexual indulgence.

Richard's immediate world, not that foreign country controlled by whites, is overwhelmingly feminine. Male contacts are gone, except for occasional encounters with uncles. The father has deserted his home, and the grandfather is lost in the memories of "The War." The uncles tend to make brief entrances and exits, following the pattern of Hoskins, quickly killed off by envious whites in Arkansas, or the unnamed new uncle, forced to flee because of unstated crimes against whites (pp. 48–49, 57–60). Thomas is the uncle who stays around somewhat longer than the others do, long enough to serve as the convenient object for Richard's mounting rebellion. The encounter with Uncle Tom is the culminating episode marking a defiance expressed earlier against a number of authority figures, all women—Richard's mother, Miss Simon, Grandmother Wilson, Aunt Addie. Women dominate in Richard's world, with the ultimate authority vested in Granny—near-white, uncompromising, unloving, and fanatical, daring Richard to desecrate her Seventh Day Adventist sabbath. The only relief from feminine piety is the pathetic school-teacher who, in a happy moment, tells an enraptured Richard about Bluebeard and his wives (p. 34). But even this delight, moved in part, no doubt, by Bluebeard's relentless war against females, is short-lived. Granny puts a stop to such sinning, not recognizing, of course, the working out of the law of compensation.

Richard's odyssey takes him from the black world to the white—from the problems of home and family to new and even more formidable difficulties. The movement is outward into the world, to confront an environment that is not controlled by Granny, though it provides much that contributes to an explanation of Granny's behavior. Richard's life among blacks emphasizes two kinds of struggle. One is simply the battle for physical existence, the need for food, clothing, shelter, and protection that is the overwhelming concern of the early pages of *Black Boy*. The second grows out of Richard's deeply felt desire to acquire his own male identity, a sense of self apart from a family that exerts increasing pressure upon this growing black boy to behave properly, to experience Christian conversion, and to accept guidance from his (mostly female) elders. Survival in two senses, then, is the dominant theme, one which does not change when he leaves the black community. The terms are the same though the landscape is new. Richard desperately seeks employment in white neighborhoods and in the downtown business districts in order to contribute to the support of his family. He discovers, when he does so, that the demand to accommodate becomes even more insistent and less flexible than that exerted by his own family.

The difference is that the stakes are higher. Richard thinks he must find a job, any job, to earn a living. This awareness represents a step beyond the simple dependence that moves a small boy to complain, "Mama, I'm hungry" (p. 13). If he does not find work, Richard feels that he has failed his family in an essential way and made its survival precarious. Though his independence in the black world leads to harsh sanctions—threats, bed without supper, whippings—he is not prepared for the infinitely greater severity of the white world. It is cruel, calculating, and sadistic.

Richard never doubts that he will survive the lashings received from his mother, Granny, and assorted aunts and uncles, but he does question his ability to endure exposure to whites. The ways of white folks are capricious and almost uniformly malignant. Richard understands that the penalty for nonconformity, down to the way a black boy walks or holds his head, is not simply a sore body, but death. When Richard gives up a good job with an optical company, with a chance, according to his boss, to become something more than a menial worker, he does so because of the opposition exhibited by whites who think he aspires to do "*white man's work.*" Richard confides to his boss when he leaves the factory: "I'm scared. . . . They would kill me" (p. 168).

From the woman who inquires of Richard, looking for yet another job, "Boy, do you steal?" (p. 128), to the two young men who attempt to arrange for Richard to fight another black boy for the amusement of an assembly of whites (pp. 209–10), we witness an unrelieved set of abuses. Certainly omission of some mitigating circumstances and artful distortion are involved in this bitter report. Richard is gradually introduced to a white world that grows progressively more dominant, divisive, and corrupting concerning the black life that serves it. Richard understands fully what is expected of him:

> I began to marvel at how smoothly the black boys acted out the roles that the white race had mapped out for them. Most of them were not conscious of living a special, separate, stunted way of life. Yet I know that in some period of their growing up—a period that they had no doubt forgotten—there had been developed in them a delicate, sensitive controlling mechanism that shut off their minds and emotions from all that the white race had said was taboo. (p. 172)

In Wright's South it was unthinkable for a black boy to aspire to become a lens grinder, much less to harbor the ambition to become a writer. When Richard is thoughtless enough to reveal his true aim in life to one of his white employers, the response is predictable: "You'll never be a writer. . . . Who on earth put such ideas into your nigger head?" (p. 129). Given his difficulties in adjusting to an oppressive southern system, Richard sustains his interest in writing through a monumental act of will. We are led to the inevitable conclusion that Richard must flee the South if he is to remain alive, and the desire to achieve an artistic career seems less important in light of the more basic concern for life itself.

We have every reason to suspect that the treatment of whites gains a certain strength from artistic deletion, too. Michael Fabre points out that Wright's relationship with a white family named Wall does not fit the pattern of abuse and brutal exploitation that emerges from the autobiography:

> Although *Black Boy* was designed to describe the effects of ra-
> cism on a black child, which meant omitting incidents tending
> to exonerate white persons in any way, there is no doubt that
> the Walls were liberal and generous employers. For almost two
> years Richard worked before and after class, earning three dol-
> lars a week bringing in firewood and doing the heavy clean-
> ing.[27]

Fabre adds, with reference especially to Mrs. Wall and her mother, "Since they respected his qualities as an individual, he sometimes submitted his problems and plans to them and soon considered their house a second home where he met with more understand-ing than from his own family."[28] This is not matter that reinforces a design displaying increasing difficulty for Richard as he moves outward and into contact with white society. Nor does it support Richard's growing conviction that his survival depends upon his escape from the South. The design of *Black Boy* offers an acceler-ating pattern of confrontations, taking into account both an in-crease in danger for Richard and a mounting seriousness in terms of society's estimate of his deviations. Like Big Boy, Richard must flee or die.

The narrator of *Black Boy* has three voices. The simplest records recollected events with clarity and a show of objectivity. We may be troubled by an insufficient context surrounding or an inadequate connection linking these episodes until we become aware of the suggestion of a psychological dimension for them. The incidents illustrate basic emotions: the discovery of fear and guilt, first, when fire destroys Richard's house; the experience of hate, directed this time toward the father, in killing the kitten; the satisfactions of violence, in defeating the teenage gang; the dangers of curiosity about the adult world, in Richard's early addiction to alcohol. The psyche of a child takes shape through exposure to a set of unusual traumas, and the child goes forth, as we have seen, into a world that becomes progressively more brutal and violent. Style in this way reinforces the first theme of the autobiography, survival.

It is in hearing the more complicated and lyrical second voice of the narrator that we sense for the first time another theme in the autobiography. This is the making of the artist. The world, we have been told, is cold, harsh, and cruel, a fact which makes all the more miraculous the emergence of a literary imagination destined to confront it. The bleak South, by some strange necessity, is forced to permit the blooming of a single rose. Wright expends upon the nourishment of this tender plant the care that he has given to describing the sterile soil from which it springs.

A third, didactic voice offers occasional explanations of the matters recorded by the other two. It comments at times upon the lack of love among blacks in the South, the distortions in human relationships involving blacks and whites, and corruption in the social and economic systems. At other times it advises us of the necessity for secrecy when a black boy harbors the ambition to write and explains the difficulties which he confronts when he seeks to serve an apprenticeship to his art. Despite formidable opposition and the danger of complete isolation, this ambition lives and forces the growth of Richard's imaginative powers.

We do not begin simply with the statement of the intention to become an artist. We start, rather, as Joyce does in *A Portrait of the Artist*, with the sense experience that rests behind the word. Richard's memory offers rich testimony of the capacity to feel objects of nature, small and large—and not only these. We note that accompanying the record of sensations is the tendency to translate sensation into an appropriate emotion—melancholy, nostalgia, astonishment, disdain. All of the senses achieve recognition in Richard's memory, and all combine to emphasize memories of violent experiences: the killing of the chicken, the shocking movement of the snake, the awesome golden glow on a silent night (pp. 7–8).

Apart from this basic repository of sensation and image, we sense early in Richard two other qualities just as essential to the budding artist. One is detachment, the feeling of being different from others. In the two worlds to which he is exposed, that of the family and then the more muddled arena of affairs, he rejects all efforts to moderate his apartness. Though conversion and subsequent baptism apparently point to joining the company of the saved, viewed in the conventional way, damnation is assured by the refusal to deliver the right kind of valedictory at the graduation exercises of his grammar school (p. 153). Barely passing one ritual, he flunks another. He maintains under pressure his status as an alien, so ultimately he will be free to exercise the imagination that faces the cold world.

The second quality is curiosity. His mother tells Richard that he asks too many questions. Our young hero is apparently undaunted by the fact that his insistent prying has led to one of the earliest addictions to alcohol recorded in literature. But another addiction is more serious, to the truth in the appearances about him. "Will you stop asking silly questions!" his mother commands (p. 42)—about names, about color, about the relationship between the two. Curiosity constantly leads Richard to forbidden areas more menacing than the saloon, to the mysterious privileged province of whites in Mississippi and the equally mysterious restriction of the blacks.

A neat form of inversion is involved in the development of Richard's artistic talent. We note that the qualities supporting and sustaining the growing boy's imagination are just those preventing a successful adjustment to life in the South. To achieve a tolerable existence, not even a comfortable one, Richard must have firm relationships with the members of his family and with his neighbors and peers; to survive in the larger, white-dominated society he must accept without questioning the inflexible system of southern mores and customs. Richard, rejecting these imperatives, responds to the demands of his own imagination. Richard's sensations in nature anticipate a discovery just as valuable and far-reaching. This is literature itself. Of the encounter with *Bluebeard* Richard says, "My sense of life deepened." He recalls, further, a total emotional response, emphasized, no doubt, by the background of an unresponding family, and he realizes that he stands on the threshold of a "gateway to a forbidden and enchanting land" (p. 36). So, early, the opposition is clear. On the one hand is the bleak environment frowning upon any activity of the imagination, whether passive or active, and on the other a determined Richard who will not be turned aside. His reading would be done in secret, a clandestine activity abetted by delivering racist newspapers and borrowing the library card of a compliant white man. There is no evidence that he discussed his reading with anyone, black or white. In Memphis, when he was able to patronize secondhand bookstores and to buy magazines like *Harper's*, *Atlantic Monthly*, and *American Mercury*, his tastes reflected the shape of his early conditioning (p. 198). He admired the great liberators, the destroyers of provincial and private worlds like the one that oppressed him: Mencken in a *Book of Prefaces* and *Prejudices*; Sinclair Lewis in *Main Street* and *Babbitt*; Theodore Dreiser in *Sister Carrie* and *Jennie Gerhardt* (pp. 217–19).

It might be said that Richard has the loneliness of a naturalistic hero, of McTeague or of Carrie Meeber. Theirs are worlds in which no one talks to anyone else, worlds entirely given over to the expression of power. One person's drive pitted against that of another, and the consequence of the struggle has more to do with heredity or chemistry than with persuasion. Richard's behavior, much like that of a character created by Norris or Dreiser, though it is not governed by the tight probability of fiction, carries constantly the solemn and overwhelming weight of the universe. He cannot say "sir" without acquiescing to the ever-present power of the white man, and he cannot read Mencken without the satisfaction that he has triumphed over a hostile white South through subterfuge and trickery.

Richard's commitment to write precipitates confrontations. As we have seen, his honest admission of this aspiration to one white female employer results in bitter ridicule, and Richard feels, despite the pressures of his situation, that his ego has been assaulted. His first publication, "The Voodoo of Hell's Half-Acre," is little more than the crude rendering of the stuff of *Flynn's Detective Weekly*, but Richard discovers that printing it is an act of defiance, further separating him from the world that surrounds him, both black and white (p. 146).

Richard does not intend to restrict his range to any half acre, though his first is identified as "Hell." His province would be the real world around him. True, it is sometimes not to be distinguished from the subject area defined by his first literary effort. At a very young age Richard sees "elephants" moving across the land—not real "elephants," but convicts in a chain gang, and the child's awe is prompted by the unfortunate confusion of elephant and zebra (p. 52). An inauspicious beginning, perhaps, but the pattern of applying his imagination to his immediate surroundings is firmly set. Later, Richard says more soberly that he rejects religion because it ignores immediate reality. His faith, predictably, must be wedded to "common realities of life" (p. 100), anchored in the sensations of his body and in what his mind could grasp. This is, we see, an excellent credo for an artist, but a worthless one for a black boy growing to maturity in Mississippi.

Another piece of evidence announcing Richard's talent is the compulsion to make symbols of the details of his everyday experience. This faculty is early demonstrated in his tendency to generalize from sensational experience, to define an appropriate emotion to associate with his feelings. A more highly developed example is Richard's reaction to his mother's illness and sufferings, representative for him in later years of the poverty, the ignorance, the helplessness of black life in Mississippi. And it is based on the generalizing process that Richard is a black boy, any black boy, experiencing childhood, adolescence, and early manhood in the South.

Richard leaves the South. He must, to survive as a man and

to develop as an artist. By the time we reach the end of the narrative, these two drives have merged. We know, as well, that the South will never leave Richard, never depart from the rich imagination that developed despite monumental opposition. We have only the final promise that Richard will someday understand the region that has indelibly marked him.

Richard's ultimate liberation, and his ultimate triumph, will be the ability to face the dreadful experience in the South and to record it. At the end of *A Portrait of the Artist as a Young Man*, the facts of experience have become journal items for the artist.[29] At the conclusion of *Invisible Man*, Ellison's unnamed narrator can record the blues of his black life, with the accompaniment of extraordinary psychedelic effects. Stephen Dedalus is on his way to becoming an artist; Ellison's hero promises to climb out of his hole, half-prepared, at least, to return to mundane life.[30] The conclusion of *Black Boy* is less positive and more tentative. True, Richard has made it; he has whipped the devils of the South, black and white. But he has left us with a feeling that is less than happy. He has yet to become an artist. Then, we realize with a start that what we have read is not simply the statement of a promise, its background and its development, but its fulfillment. Wright has succeeded in reconstructing the reality that was for a long time perhaps too painful to order, and that reconstruction may be Wright's supreme artistic achievement, *Black Boy*.

Notes

1. New York: Harper, 1940. Dorothy Canfield Fisher in the introduction writes that the "novel plumbs blacker depths of human experience than American literature has yet had, comparable only to Dostoievski's revelation of human misery in wrongdoing" (p. x).

2. The full title is *Black Boy: A Record of Childhood and Youth* (New York: Harper, 1945). Dorothy Fisher in the introductory note calls Wright's work "the honest, dreadful, heartbreaking story of a Negro childhood and youth" (p. vii), without referring to its art or even its place in an American literary tradition.

3. "Life and Letters: Richard Wright Reappraised," *Atlantic Monthly* 225 (March 1970): 127–32.

4. *American Hunger* (New York: Harper & Row) was published in 1977. It is not the whole autobiography but the second part, the continuation of *Black Boy*. Michel Fabre in the afterword provides an accurate brief history of the decision to publish only the first section in 1945. See pp. 143–44.

5. *Atlantic Monthly* 174 (August 1944): 61–70; (September 1944): 48–56.

6. Fabre, afterword, *American Hunger*, pp. 143–44.

7. W. E. B. Du Bois, "Richard Wright Looks Back," *New York Herald Tribune*, March 4, 1945, sec. 5, p. 2.

8. The three are *The Souls of Black Folk: Essays and Sketches* (Chicago: McClurg, 1903), *Darkwater: Voices from within the Veil* (New York: Harcourt, Brace, 1920), and *Dusk of Dawn: An Essay toward an Autobiography of a Race Concept* (New York: Harcourt, Brace, 1940).

9. Chapter 4, "Of the Meaning of Progress," in Du Bois, *The Souls of Black Folk*, pp. 60–74.

10. "Richard Wright's Blues," *Antioch Review* 5 (June 1945): 202; reprinted in Ralph Ellison, *Shadow and Act* (New York: Random House, 1964).

11. Wright wrote Edward Aswell, his editor at Harper's, on August 10, 1944, suggesting *Black Boy* as a title for the book. He added, for emphasis, that *Black Boy* was "not only a title but also a kind of heading to the whole general theme" (Fabre, afterword, *American Hunger*, p. 144).

12. Wright comments on this commitment in *Black Boy*: "I had once tried to write, had once reveled in feeling, had let my crude imagination roam, but the impulse to dream had been slowly beaten out of me by experience. Now it surged up again and I hungered for books, new ways of looking and seeing" (p. 218).

13. Ibid., p. 220.

14. Between 1897 and 1915 Du Bois edited fifteen studies on the condition and status of blacks in America. These volumes represented the proceedings of the Annual Conference on the Negro Problem, organized by Du Bois and held at Atlanta University.

15. Ellison, "Richard Wright's Blues," p. 202.

16. *Native Son*, pp. 4–5.

17. Thoreau is precise about the length of his actual stay, despite the fact that the events of *Walden* fall within the design of a single year: "The present was my next experiment . . . for convenience, putting the

experience of two years into one." Henry David Thoreau, *Walden*, ed. Sherman Paul (Boston: Houghton Mifflin, 1957), p. 58.

18. Franklin refers in this way to his neglect of Miss Read, to whom he was engaged, during a period spent in London: "This was another of the great errata of my life." "Autobiography," in Benjamin Franklin, *Autobiography and Other Writings*, ed. R. B. Nye (Boston: Houghton Mifflin, 1958), p. 38.

19. See Michel Fabre, *The Unfinished Quest of Richard Wright* (New York: Morrow 1973), pp. 1–17.

20. Ibid., p. 533.

21. Another footnote by Fabre in *Unfinished Quest* suggests an additional dimension for Addie, who "too, was not, spared in *Black Boy*. She reacted rather well to reading the book—she stated that if Richard wrote in that way, it was to support his family" (p. 533).

22. Ibid., p. 39.

23. Ibid., p. 48.

24. E. R. Embree describes, in *Thirteen against the Odds* (New York: Viking, 1944), Wright's attitude toward his education in Jackson: "He [Wright] remembers the Smith-Robinson school with some gratitude. The teachers tried their best to pump learning into the pupils" (p. 27).

25. Fabre, *Unfinished Quest*, p. 39.

26. Ibid., p. 43.

27. Ibid., pp. 46–47.

28. Ibid., p. 47.

29. See James Joyce, *A Portrait of the Artist as a Young Man* (New York: New American Library, 1955), pp. 195–96.

30. Ellison's narrator states his final position with some care: "Thus, having tried to give pattern to the chaos which lives within the pattern of your certainties, I must come out, I must emerge." *Invisible Man* (New York: New American Library, 1952), p. 502.

Literacy and Ascent

Richard Wright's Black Boy

ROBERT B. STEPTO

◆　◆　◆

T H I S [E S S A Y]—which could be entitled "Reading, Writing, and Ascent"—focuses on another strain of indebtedness in [*Black Boy*], one that is rooted far more in turn-of-the-century literature than in what came before. The strain to which I refer links *Black Boy* to antedating texts such as Sutton Elbert Grigg's *Imperium in Imperio*, Du Bois's *The Souls of Black Folk*, and Johnson's *The Autobiography of an Ex-Coloured Man*, and establishes *Black Boy* as an antedating text for many recent narratives, including Ellison's *Invisible Man* and Toni Morrison's *The Bluest Eye*. What all these narratives share (or rather, participate in) is a primary scene in Afro-American letters: the schoolroom episode, which is often accompanied by its chief variant, the graduation episode. The significance of this scene has less to do with the extraordinary frequency of its appearance or even with its "logical" place in a prose literature dominated by autobiographical and *Bildungsroman* impulses, and more to do with how it characterizes and shapes—in literary terms—a discernible period in Afro-American literary history. Schoolroom and graduation episodes in Afro-American

literature begin to assume their proper stature when we recall
not only the laws and race rituals that enforced a people's illit-
eracy (vis-à-vis the written word) but also the body of literature,
including most obviously the slave narratives, that expresses again
and again the quest for freedom *and* literacy achieved regardless
of the odds, regardless of the lack of sanctioned opportunities,
such as school attendance. When familiar images in the early
narrative literature, such as that of a Frederick Douglass or a
William Wells Brown having to dupe white urchins in order to
learn the rudiments of reading and ciphering, give way to fresh
if not altogether joyous expressions of black youths in one-room
schoolhouses, high schools, institutes, colleges, and even univer-
sities, then we may say truly that a primary configuration in the
tradition is being systematically revoiced and that these expressions are almost singlehandedly creating a new contour in the
tradition's history. To place *The Souls of Black Folk* or *Black Boy* in
this contour, for example, is to say more about either text (especially about their relations to one another) than can be said
when they are relegated to categories largely imposed by other
disciplines, such as "literature of accommodation" and "literature
of protest."

One point to be made regarding Richard Wright's participation
in these activities is that his greatest novel, *Native Son*, is totally
bereft of any schoolroom or graduation episode—unless one
wishes (somewhat perversely) to assign those properties to the
cell or courtroom scenes, or to Bigger's "tutorials" with Attorney
Max. In contrast, *Black Boy*'s middle chapters are one sustained
schoolroom episode; furthermore, the graduation episode that
completes chapter VIII is unquestionably a major event in the
narrative, and perhaps *the* event young Richard seeks when he
earlier confides that he is "waiting for some event, some word,
some act, some circumstance to furnish the impetus" for his flight
from what he calls elsewhere "that southern swamp of despair
and violence." The resulting contrast between the two volumes
should not be viewed in any qualitative way—for example, the
absence of the schoolroom scene from *Native Son* does not cate-
gorically make it a superior or inferior work of literature. But it

should be examined, nevertheless, if for no other reason than to receive its suggestion of the full reach of the Afro-American landscape charted by Wright's oeuvre. Once this reach or territory is explored (and the space between Bigger's world and Wright's persona's world is indeed of continental proportions), the glories and failures of Wright's transtextual artistic vision become newly manifest. The glory is primarily and fundamentally the territory itself, a space full of nightmare and misery that is finally bounded only by the seemingly limitless horizons of living and knowing. The failure is essentially that Wright's antipodal construction of the landscape unwittingly positions his supreme fiction of himself—not just as a man or even as an articulate survivor, but as an artist—*within* an antipode, and hence removes it from whatever mediating postures might be available to him. Much has already been said about this particular failure or dilemma; Ralph Ellison and George Kent explore this issue in their own way when they remark respectively that "Wright could imagine Bigger, but Bigger could not possibly imagine Richard Wright," and that Wright's "deepest consciousness is that of the exaggerated Westerner." My interest here, however, lies less with investigating Wright's resulting posture as an artist and more with exploring the way stations and stretches of road that constitute the pathway to whatever posture Wright's persona in *Black Boy* achieves. And it seems clear that the persona's school experiences provide a proper place to begin.

Since the world of *Black Boy* is so relentlessly hostile, we should not be surprised to discover that most of young Richard's learning situations are pockets of fear and misery. Certain features of the schoolroom scene, such as the persona's first efforts to acquire a (written and spoken) voice, are sustained here and there, providing a few bright moments. However, when these features occur, they are usually contextualized in the narrative as the spoils of bitter battles; their piercing light may be attributed as much to the flash of weapons as to the lamp of learning. Wright's persona is so embattled in his school experiences partly because, until he enters the Jim Hill School at the age of twelve, most of his schooling occurs at home or in classrooms that are formidable extensions of that horrific and inhibiting domestic world. When Ella (who is, we recall, a schoolteacher) clandestinely tells young Richard the spirited tale of Bluebeard, transporting him to new worlds beyond whatever he had previously dreamt and felt, the porch where they sit becomes momentarily a schoolroom complete with globe, primer, and, most important, a teacher sensitive to a child's hunger for knowledge. But that porch is first and foremost—as well as finally—Granny Wilson's porch, and Granny, with her particular ideas about the extraordinary reach of the Devil's hand, seems always just beyond the doorway, ready to pounce upon any "mischief" invading her domain. Another construction of this situation is offered when Aunt Addie returns from the Seventh Day Adventist Religious School in Huntsville to open her own church school. Unfortunately, young Richard has no choice but to matriculate there. From the start, it is clear that things could not be worse if the class were taught by Granny Wilson herself: Richard and Addie square off right away, and when the battle of wills leads to a pitched free-for-all, replete with biting and kicking, in which Richard brandishes a kitchen knife in much the same fashion that he will later grab a razor blade in each fist to ward off his Uncle Tom, we cannot possibly be surprised to learn that Addie stopped calling on Richard in class and that "consequently [he] stopped studying."

Not all of Richard's "home learning" in *Black Boy* is this violent or unfulfilled. The rare moments of learning from kin are provided by his mother, usually during those brief interludes when they are living neither with his father nor with Granny Wilson— the prime representatives of the narrative's oppressive exterior and interior spaces. Quite typically, given Wright's drive to achieve literacy vis-à-vis the word, the best example of his mother in a teaching role involves diction—the choice of certain words for certain conditions and circumstances. And, quite appropriately, given the violent world of the narrative, the words he learns to use are "whip" and "beat" and, less directly, "boy" and "man":

When word circulated among the black people of the neighborhood that a "black" boy had been severely beaten by a "white" man, I felt that the "white" man had had a right to beat the "black" boy, for I naively assumed that the "white" man must have been the "black" boy's father. And did not all fathers, like my father, have the right to beat their children?

. . . But when my mother told me that the "white" man was not the father of the "black" boy, was no kin to him at all, I was puzzled.

"Then why did the 'white' man whip the 'black' boy?" I asked my mother.

"The 'white' man did not *whip* the 'black' boy," my mother told me. "He *beat* the 'black' boy."

"But why?"

"You're too young to understand." [21]

To be sure, young Richard does not understand completely—but when does one ever pick up a grain of truth, in or out of school, and understand it completely upon first hearing? Sad as it may be, it is through exchanges such as this one that young Richard is taught about his environment, his place in it, and about *how* words mean as well as *what* they mean. Although his mother is unquestionably a part of the domestic structure afflicting and oppressing him, she is also, possibly because she is his mother, the best teacher his circumstances afford him: she explains words, she tells him stories, she helps him learn how to read. For this reason—and perhaps, too, because his semi-invalid mother often appears to be as ensnared by the household as he is—young Richard cares for her, is not violent with her, and grieves for her in his own stolid way during her many illnesses. Still, there is an underlying tension between Richard's deep feelings for his mother and his compulsion—based not on whim or fancy, but on a rather accurate assessment of his circumstances—to take his neophyte stories and sketches outside the home, to show them to others including, in the first instance, an incredulous neighbor woman who most certainly turns out not to be the surrogate mother, aunt, or grandmother that Richard is obviously searching for. The abiding presence of this dilemma offers one more reason why Richard must leave the South—and take his mother with him. While flight may not allow mother and son to recapture those special moments when the home was a site of learning, it will at least extract them from Granny's lair and allow them to begin again.

Significant schooling outside the home environment in *Black Boy* begins only when young Richard enters the Jim Hill Public School. The only earlier public school experience reported in the narrative occurs in Memphis, shortly after his father disappears. Richard's brief report serves mainly to depict the point of departure for his ascent, first and most immediately in his school world and then in the larger circumferences of his life beyond the South:

> I began school at Howard Institute at a later age than was usual; my mother had not been able to buy me the necessary clothes to make me presentable. The boys of the neighborhood took me to school the first day and when I reached the edge of the school grounds I became terrified, wanted to return home, wanted to put it off. But the boys simply took my hand and pulled me inside the building. I was frightened speechless and the other children had to identify me, tell the teacher my name and address. I sat listening to pupils recite, knowing and understanding what was being said and done, but utterly incapable of opening my mouth when called upon. The students around me seemed so sure of themselves that I despaired of ever being able to conduct myself as they did. [21]

In this way, in a context removed from the domestic interior, Wright's persona initiates a motif that we know from the slave narratives: the ascent to find a voice which can, among other things, guide conduct and name itself. But the ascent is not immediately forthcoming; all of the episodes described above involving Granny Wilson and Aunt Addie—episodes marking young Richard's forced return to the domestic interior—intercede between his all-too-few days at Howard Institute and his three years at the Jim Hill School. When he finally reenters the school world, his longing to begin the ascent has become an unfathomable energy, and his hunger for learning and for exploring the realm beyond Granny Wilson's doorstep is even more acute than his perpetual desire for food. Indeed, as he tells of his first days at Jim Hill School and of his willingness to go without his usual miserable fare at home in order to see "a world leap to life," he remarks, "To starve in order to learn about my environment was irrational, but so were my hungers."

Although this may suggest that the school world of *Black Boy* is, in comparison to the narrative's other structural spaces, a kind of paradise, such is hardly the case. In fact, the school world is truly the second circle of Wright's southern hell, just as the oppressing domestic interior is the first circle, and the white world of the narrative, to which young Richard will be introduced shortly, is the third. The school world is not as physically violent as the domestic interior, but it has its own array of punishments and afflictions, which display themselves fully in both of the signal episodes in which Wright's persona takes a symbolic step toward freedom and literacy.

In the first episode, young Richard writes a short story ("The Voodoo of Hell's Half-Acre") which the mature Wright describes in retrospect as being "crudely atmospheric, emotional, intuitively psychological." The youth instinctively shows it to someone outside the hostile environments of home and school, the editor of the local Negro newspaper. The happy result is that the story is printed—young Richard has indeed come far from that day when he shared his first sketch with a neighbor. But any joy or inspiration that he experiences is quickly stifled by what he calls elsewhere "the tribe in which [I] lived and of which [I was] a part." After family, schoolmates, and teachers pummel him with their questions and condemnations, he is left thoroughly alone and abused—"I felt that I had committed a crime"—but charged all the more with the self-generated energy needed to continue his ascent. It is quite significant that the episode ends with Wright's persona's first expression of the North as a destination and a symbolic space and that his emerging fantasy of what he will do there involves acts of literacy on a grand scale: "I dreamed of going north and writing books, novels. The North symbolized to me all that I had not felt and seen; it had no relation whatever to what actually existed. Yet, by imagining a place where everything was possible, I kept hope alive in me" [147]. These imaginings keep young Richard valiantly on the move for many years, but their immediate and much-needed effect is to offer him enough resilience to endure another year of tribal rigors at home and at school.

During the next year (and chapter) of the narrative, young Richard takes his second symbolic step toward freedom and literacy while at Jim Hill School, and that step is described in the graduation episode. While the first step involving his storywriting may be said to be an indebted and inverted rendering of the "ex-coloured man's" reception as a youthful artist within his community, the graduation episode is a comparably indebted and inverted expression of many prior moments in the literature, but especially perhaps of that day in 1841 when Frederick Douglass rose to the podium and found his voice in Nantucket. In each of Wright's episodes, his inversion of antecedent expressions is not total—"The Voodoo of Hell's Half-Acre" is probably no less flawed than the "ex-coloured man's" youthful interpretations of romantic melodies, and Wright's persona's graduation speech is certainly no worse than Bernard Belgrave's in *Imperium in Imperio* or Shiny's in *The Autobiography*. But that is not the point. It is rather that Wright seems intent upon revising certain abiding expressions within the literary tradition of communal succor and of potential immersion in community in order to place *Black Boy* within the ranks of the narrative of ascent. Put another way, his effort is to create a persona who experiences major moments of literacy, personal freedom, and personal growth while in a kind of bondage, and yet who maintains in a very clear-headed way his vision of a higher literacy and a better world.

As one might expect, the heart of the graduation episode is not the delivery of speech or its reception—that would suggest that communal bonds between speaker and audience are possible and that the persona is satisfied with the stage of literacy he has achieved. Rather, the episode focuses on the series of tempestuous events that precede the "great day." Of these, none is more important than young Richard's conversation with the principal of the Jim Hill School. The scene that ensues should be familiar to students of Afro-American literature, because the principal is clearly an intermediate manifestation of a character type most visibly inaugurated by Jean Toomer in *Cane*'s figure of Hanley, and most formidably completed (for the moment) by Ralph Ellison in *Invisible Man*'s Bledsoe. In that scene young Richard is forced to choose between his principal and his principle: whether to accept and read a speech ghostwritten by a "bought" man, or to go ahead with a speech written by himself, on his own and probably in the same tattered but secretly dear notebook that produced "The Voodoo of Hell's Half-Acre." He chooses the latter course, and there ensues a predictable response among the tribe—from the principal on down to his schoolmates and, at the level of his home life, his worn-out and retired kinsman Uncle Tom. After the barrage of assaults and cajolings, including bribes, Richard doggedly pursues his righteous course and describes the resulting event in this way:

> On the night of graduation I was nervous and tense; I rose and faced the audience and my speech rolled out. When my voice stopped there was some applause. I did not care if they liked it or not; I was through. Immediately, even before I left the platform, I tried to shut all memory of the event from me. A few of my classmates managed to shake my hand as I pushed toward the door, seeking the street. Somebody invited me to a party and I did not accept. I did not want to see any of them again. I walked home, saying to myself: The hell with it! With almost seventeen years of baffled living behind me, I faced the world in 1925. [156]

Several aspects of this statement interest me greatly, and I would like to offer two additional quotations from other sources by way of beginning to remark upon them. The first is quite recognizably from the 1845 Douglass *Narrative*:

But, while attending an anti-slavery convention at Nantucket, on the 11th of August, 1841, I felt strongly moved to speak. ... It was a severe cross, and I took it up reluctantly. The truth was, I felt myself a slave, and the idea of speaking to white people weighed me down. I spoke but a few moments, when I felt a degree of freedom, and said what I desired with considerable ease. From that time until now, I have been engaged in pleading the cause of my brethren—with what success, and with what devotion, I leave those acquainted with my labors to decide.

The second quotation, as much a part of the tradition as the first, is from Langston Hughes's "The Negro Writer and the Racial Mountain," published in the *Nation* in 1926, within a year after Wright's persona made his commencement speech at the Jim Hill School:

We younger Negro artists who create now intend to express our individual dark-skinned selves without fear or shame. If white people are pleased we are glad. If they are not, it doesn't matter. ... If colored people are pleased we are glad. If they are not, their displeasure doesn't matter either. We build our temples for tomorrow, strong as we know how, and we stand on top of the mountain, free within ourselves.

By citing these very different passages, I want to suggest that the voice Wright's persona assumes—the voice found and honed presumably through experiences such as those surrounding and including the graduation—is very much in the Afro-American heroic strain. The hard-won freedom that Wright's persona acquires from the ordeal of the entire valedictory event is, at root, much the same as the "degree of freedom" Douglass experiences while addressing the throng. Furthermore, while Wright's persona has neither reached the top of his idea of the "racial mountain" nor designed the temple to be situated in that space (that "Blueprint" will come twelve years later), he clearly shares Hughes's conviction that one must ascend beyond the "low ground" of oppres-

sive—interracial and intraracial—social structures to gain one's
voice on one's own terms and, in that sense, be free. Like Du Bois
before them, Wright and Hughes both seek the heights of a "Pis-
gah" soaring above the "dull . . . hideousness" of a structural to-
pography that is racially both black and white.

What is new about Wright's rendering of this familiar event is
not the voice achieved, but the positioning of the event in the
narrative itself. Unlike Douglass, Wright is not trying to end his
narrative; instead, he is attempting to move his persona from one
world of the narrative to another. He does not want to suggest
(as Douglass does) that the achievement of voice may yield even
a fleeting sense of personal ease and of community, for that
would disruptively suggest that his persona has found a measure
of comfort and stability in the very world he is about to leave.
And so Wright's persona moves on with his stride unbroken—
handshakes are barely acknowledged, invitations to parties are
cast aside—and with only one small anchor fixing the occasion
in official time: he mentions the year, and it is 1925. One notes
this latter point partly because, in accord with the Du Boisian
model in *The Souls*, few dates are recorded in *Black Boy*, and partly
because 1925 is such a watershed year in Afro-American literature.
What this suggests about the graduation episode in *Black Boy* is
that Wright is concerned not only about positioning the event in
the narrative itself, but also about placing the event in Afro-
American literary history. At the very time when the New Negro
"renaissance" was under full sway in Harlem (*The New Negro*, edited by Alain Locke, made the pages of *Survey Graphic* in 1925) and,
tangentially, in places such as Washington, D.C. (let us not forget
Georgia Douglas Johnson, Jean Toomer, Sterling Brown, and Edward "Duke" Ellington), Richard Wright was belatedly but tri-
umphantly graduating from the Jim Hill School and, according
to the exquisite fiction of his personal history, thinking much the
same thoughts that a bona fide renaissance hero (Langston
Hughes) would publish within a year.

Wright gets the maximum mileage out of the graduation episode, and he does so in accord with his particular vision of how
he must revise and at the same time honor tradition in order to

assume a place within it. His revision of Douglass's model episode allows his persona to travel on, having achieved a voice and vision comparable to Douglass's; and with his revision of Afro-American literary history vis-à-vis 1925 he makes a place for himself within that history well before any of his major texts were written—let alone, saw print. With these ingenious undertakings completed, it is hard to believe that *Black Boy* has not run its course—although, in a very real sense, it has only just begun.

Editors' note: Page references to *Black Boy* supplied by the editors in brackets are taken from the 1945 Harper edition.

An Apprenticeship to Life and Art

Narrative Design in Wright's Black Boy

JOHN O. HODGES

◆ ◆ ◆

THE EARLY YEARS of the twentieth century were marked by race riots, lynchings, and the revival of the Ku Klux Klan. The Klan was energetically gathering "qualified persons" under its banner of "Native, Protestant, Supreme," and by 1924 this organization could claim a membership exceeding four million individuals. The South, of course, with its rather large black population, became the center of the nation's unrest and disharmony.

In a statement before the Southern Conference for Education in 1904, Bishop Charles Betts Galloway presented the case for this region: "In the South there will never be any social mingling of the races. Whether it be prejudice or pride of race, there is a middle wall of partition which will not be broken down."[1] Clearly marked signs of "White Only" and "For Colored" were strategically located to make sure that all knew their proper place, for the South was prepared to take stern measures against those who, for whatever reason, attempted to traverse the racial line.

This is a South to which few now, perhaps, would cling. But it is the South in which Richard Wright (born September 4, 1908) spent his boyhood, and it is this image of the South, with its brutality, fear, and deprivation, that haunts almost all of his fiction, whether the setting be the deep South or Chicago's South Side. So deeply wounded was he by the injustices of his youth that by 1945, when *Black Boy* appeared, he could still render those days of fear, hunger, and violence with remarkable vividness. And throughout his various writings, whether in fiction or in the polemical essay, he attempted to give voice to those, who, like himself, had suffered under the extreme pressures of injustice and racism. "Being a Negro," Wright once said, "has to do with the American scene, with race hate, rejection, ignorance, segregation, slavery, murder, fiery crosses, and fear."[2] These are the evils which mark the bleak landscape of Wright's *Black Boy* and of several of his other works, most notably *Uncle Tom's Children* and *Native Son*. Wright certainly had, in these two earlier works, achieved a measure of success in calling attention to the inimical effects of racial injustice and prejudice on the human personality. But in *Black Boy* he achieves even greater success. For here the themes of fear, hunger, and deprivation are related to his own development and therefore attain an immediacy and poignancy unlike that found in either *Uncle Tom's Children* or *Native Son*.

As the story of a boy's journey from ignorance to experience, *Black Boy* possesses significant features of the classical *Bildungsroman*,[3] a work which recounts a young man's education or character formation. According to Roy Pascal in his book *The German Novel*, the *Bildungsroman* is the "story of the formation of a character up to the moment when he ceases to be self-centered and becomes society-centered, thus beginning to form his true Self."[4] And *Black Boy* is the story of a boy whose selfhood must be forged in the crucible of a hostile society which is determined to suppress any positive assertion of personhood. Since Richard is interested in pursuing a literary career, the restrictions which his society places upon him become all the more serious. *Black Boy*, then, like other exemplary works in the genre (such as Goethe's *Wilhelm Meister*, Keller's *Grüne Heinrich*, and Joyce's *Portrait of the Artist*), depicts the arduous pilgrimage of the embattled artist in a restrictive environment.

Like Keller's Heinrich Lee, young Richard "hungers"—both physically and spiritually—for the opportunity to release his creative potential. For Heinrich Lee the urge is to become a great painter, and during the long days of his apprenticeship he encounters problems similar to those which beset Richard. Parallels are also to be found in Goethe's *Lehrjahre* (the volume of *Wilhelm Meister* which treats Wilhelm's apprenticeship to the German theater) and in Joyce's *Portrait of the Artist*, a work which Wright knew quite well.[5]

But while *Black Boy* adheres to the structural design of the *Bildungsroman*, the book goes significantly beyond the genre's usual theme of a boy's awakening self-consciousness as he apprehends the mysteries of the world about him. In *Black Boy*, Richard must win self-knowledge in a society that is not only repressive and restrictive but profoundly antagonistic as well. And this antagonism is experienced not only in his effort to become a writer but at every level, even at the fundamental level of human survival itself. There is also, in *Black Boy*, a fraternal dimension unlike anything we find in the typical *Bildungsroman*. For Wright attempts to call attention not only to his own difficult journey but to that of other black youths who attempted to take hold of the meaning of their lives in the hostile atmosphere of the deep American South of a few generations ago.

In the course of a radio interview in the spring of 1945, Wright set forth very candidly what had been his basic intention in *Black Boy*:

> I wrote the book to tell a series of incidents strung through my childhood, but the main desire was to render a judgment on my environment because I felt the necessity to. That judgment was this: the environment the South creates is too small to nourish human beings. . . . I wanted to lend, give my tongue to the voiceless Negro boys.[6]

Indeed, the self-portrait which emerges is of one whose experience embraced the worst hardships suffered by blacks under the southern caste system. And, inevitably, his purpose required him to suppress certain details of his life and to exaggerate others, in order that the narrative design might stress the ordeals experienced by a typical southern black. His account, though autobiographical, "would be more than that; he would use himself as a symbol of all the brutality wreaked upon the black man by the Southern environment."[7]

The writing of *Black Boy*, therefore, was meant to serve at least two purposes: that of enabling Wright to retrace his steps in order to understand himself and to understand where he stood in relationship to the black community and that of creating a platform from which a judgment might be pronounced on the southern white society which blighted the hopes and aspirations of its black youth. My intention here is to demonstrate how Wright, by carefully designing and narrating the story of his life, attempts to accomplish simultaneously these distinct objectives within the narrative structure of his autobiography.

Wright's twofold objective of reporting on his own experience and of exposing the brutality and insensitivity of the South required him to adopt a rather elaborate narrative strategy. He had to present the story from the perspective of an average black boy victimized and brutalized by his experiences in the South, while at the same time accounting for the fact that those very experiences, though daunting for so many, had actually goaded him toward significant achievement. Furthermore, he had to devise a method whereby he could criticize what he considered to be shortcomings in his own people, while also holding the white South responsible for those shortcomings. Wright's intention required him to exploit fully the tension between past and present, between the boy who experiences and the mature author who interprets.

Therefore, although the account appears to be presented from the perspective of a first-person narrator, we detect two distinct voices, two "I's." On the one hand, we have the "I" of the narrative present where the account is presented from the point of view of the boy's own developing consciousness as he confronts each new experience. On the other hand, we have the "I" of the writer as he imposes his present state of consciousness on the events of the narrative. This latter type of "telling" narration (in Wayne Booth's sense)[8] makes it possible for the writer to interpret and even to criticize the protagonist's actions from the standpoint of his (the writer's) present knowledge of the outcome of those events. Furthermore, the "intrusive" narrator attempts to convince his audience of the soundness or unsoundness of the boy's actions.

Indeed, even when the narration is filtered through the consciousness of the boy, we recognize the author's hand, for young Richard is made to speak words and to handle metaphors and symbols which he, because of his immaturity, could not possibly have understood. So in this sense, too, the protagonist is made to speak for the author. Yet this type of narration succeeds in ways that the intrusive narration does not, because once the author has prepared the script for the ensuing action, he appears to withdraw from the scene and allows the hero to occupy the center of the stage. From this point of view the audience is able to judge firsthand not only the conduct of the protagonist who speaks the language and attempts to manipulate the symbols of the author, but also the attitude of the author toward his protagonist. And since the protagonist speaks for the author, we are actually determining the author's *present* attitude toward his past.

Perhaps one of the most effective means of charting Richard's growth of consciousness is through the author's use of a "naive" hero, a technique which is commonly associated with the *Bildungsroman* convention. It is only through incessant probing and at the expense of great pain and suffering that the boy begins to unlock the various secrets and mysteries of the adult world. After Granny gives him his bath, he tells her to "kiss back there," and his parents give him a stern beating. Concerning this he writes: "[I]n the future I would learn the meaning of why they had beat and denounced me."[9] And, in general, he notices that his mother becomes extremely irritated whenever he inquires about the relationship between blacks and whites. When he asks her why the family chose not to fight back when Uncle Hoskins was killed, she immediately slaps him. Or again, when he sees a black chain gang being driven by white guards (which he at first takes to be a herd of elephants), he asks his mother whether the white men ever wore stripes, to which she reluctantly replies, "sometimes," though she herself never saw any. Thus, for young Richard, "[t]he days and hours began to speak with a clearer tongue. Each new experience had a sharp meaning of its own" (p. 53).

The primary role of the naive hero, however, is to call into question those injustices which blacks and whites, because of habit and custom, dismiss all too perfunctorily. In short, the boy, in wearing the mask of the author, forces those about him—and Wright's readers as well—to examine the deeper implications of their actions. The boy, perhaps because he is ignorant of the customs of Jim Crow, is free of the bigotry and prejudice that hinder blacks and whites from achieving any stable relationships in the South. He exhibits, furthermore, a higher moral sense and a greater sensitivity than do the more mature individuals about him, and he thus becomes an adequate "voice" for revealing the hypocrisy and ruthlessness of the South during Wright's youth.

Dialogue is yet another form of narration which enables us to observe the drama of selfhood as it unfolds in the autobiography. As the youth converses with others, both blacks and whites, who are more mature and sophisticated than he, we learn much about his personality and developing consciousness, especially about how he sees himself in relation to these individuals. Here again, however, as with the other forms of narration, the portrait that we have is one which is determined more by the author's present attitudes and experiences than by any actual events in his past. Since he cannot possibly recall with absolute exactness the various exchanges he has had with others, he must search his present storehouse of words, images, and symbols for suitable metaphors of those past experiences. The author, therefore, is "free" to re-create the dialogues in a manner which best accords with his own general purpose and intention. And it is by way of Wright's effort to give his narrative a true structure—that is, to make it stand for more than a mere chronology of the major events of his life—that the various modes of narration come to play such an important role.

The whole narrative design of the book functions in conjunction with elements of structure and theme in order to produce the total effect of a boy's difficult journey from innocence to experience. It is to a closer examination of the process of this boy's education that we must now turn.

Wright recounts the crucial experiences of his youth with extraordinary poignancy, and one feels that it is his hope to make his readers at once conscious of and also in some sense prepared to take responsibility for the anguish which he and other black boys experienced in the South of his day. The boy's awakening self-consciousness evolves in stages which correspond to the three sectors of society through which he successively moves: his own household, the black community, and the larger white world. Richard's understanding of himself and of the world he inhabits increases with each new *rite de passage*, so that once he has encountered the whole of southern life, he has a clearer knowledge of who he is and of the future course his life must take.

The narrator begins the story of his life not with its beginning but with those "four-year-old days," the time when he first becomes conscious of the fear, hunger, and violence that are to plague him throughout his childhood. Wright's decision not to recount the circumstances of his birth betrays his intention to thrust young Richard's developing selfhood immediately into the center of the design.

The opening lines establish the tone of fear and despair which pervades the entire narrative. While the atmosphere of anxiety and dread stems at this point from within Richard's own household, we get the impression that it only presages the larger insecurities which he is to encounter in the outside world. Richard seems to fear his grandmother, for instance, not so much because she is a stern taskmaster, but because she is, for all intents and purposes, white: "I was dreaming of running and playing and shouting but the vivid image of Granny's old, white, wrinkled, grim face framed by a halo of tumbling black hair, lying upon a huge feather pillow, made me afraid" (p. 9). Later in his recital the narrator confides to us that, indeed, his "grandmother was as nearly white as a Negro can get without being white, which means that she was white" (p. 49). The color white, then, already begins to take on a decidedly sinister aspect, and, though Richard appears unaware of the fact at this point, it seems to have been a color which in his experience was regularly associated with restrictiveness. He is forbidden, for example, to touch the fluffy white curtains in his room. And when he finally musters enough courage to strike out against this symbol, he accidentally sets the whole house on fire, an act for which, as he says "[I was] lashed so hard and long that I lost consciousness. . . . I was lost in a fog of fear" (p. 13). Moreover, while recovering from this beating, he sees above him "wobbly white bags, like the full udders of cows, suspended from the ceiling" (p. 13). "Later on," he continues, "as I grew worse, I could see the bags in the daytime with my eyes open and I was grasped by the fear that they were going to fall and drench me in some horrible liquid" (p. 13). In using white as a symbol of fear and restriction, Wright was only further developing a theme which had earlier been a part of *Native Son* and of several of the stories in *Uncle Tom's Children*. For whether it is the white cat which attempts to corner a black rat or the white walls of Bigger's jail cell, white always seems to be a symbol of repression which threatens to imprison the Self.

The whippings this boy receives, though no doubt excessive, are meant to curb that natural curiosity which, outside the home, could result in his death. Furthermore, he is warned against asking too many questions regarding the nature of the relationship between blacks and whites. When he learns of a white man having beaten a black boy, Richard does not understand, for, as he reasons, "a paternal right is the only right that a man has to beat a child." And though his mother refuses to answer forthrightly all of the boy's queries—as he must be spared the bitter realities of his existence—the questions he raises are penetrating ones that are meant to disturb our consciences.

Richard's father is also a source of fear and anxiety. The narrator recalls: "He was the lawgiver in our family and I never laughed in his presence." Though his father's disappearance early on in his life means that he can enjoy a relatively greater degree of freedom, unfortunately it also means greater hardship for the family. There is, for example, never enough food in the house.

Indeed, he recalls: "Hunger was with us always. . . . As the days slid past the image of my father became associated with my pangs of hunger, and whenever I felt hunger I thought of him with a deep biological bitterness" (p. 22).

Although the narrator insists that he has since forgiven his father, they were "forever strangers, speaking a different language, living on vastly different planes of reality" (p. 42). While he himself has gone on to achieve some measure of success, his father remained "imprisoned by the slow flow of the seasons, by wind and rain and sun." Wright's judgment is indeed a harsh one, as he seems to attack his father for a lack of resourcefulness and courage because he permitted himself to be defeated by the pressures of the southern experience. Moreover, having by the end of the opening chapter been accounted a failure, the elder Wright from this point on plays no part in the narrative, as though the son has chosen simply to expel him from the circle of his attention.

Without the spiritual support of a father, Richard frequents bars where he learns to speak obscenities even before he can read. And worse, he declares, "I was a drunkard in my sixth year before I had begun school." His mother now not only has to provide the economic support for the family, but she has the added responsibility of teaching the boy those methods of survival on which his life depends. It is she, for example, who teaches him to fight back when he is attacked by a gang of boys in Memphis who threaten to take the money he has been given to purchase groceries.

Besides learning how to survive in the streets and taverns of Memphis, Richard has also to learn how to deal with the bitter friction which exists between the two races. While he had witnessed the beating of a black boy by a white policeman and had heard stories of violent encounters between blacks and whites, it is not until he visits Granny in Jackson that he begins to understand the seriousness of the hostility which exists between "the two races who lived side by side but never touched, it seemed, except in violence." Significantly, his first real experience of violence (apart from the harsh punishment he receives at the hands of his parents) is a vicarious one which he receives as Ella, a schoolteacher who rents a room in Granny's house, reads him one of her stories, "Bluebeard and His Seven Wives." He recalls:

> The tale made the world around me be, throb, live. As she spoke, reality changed, the look of things altered, and the world became peopled with magical presences. My sense of life deepened and the feel of things was different somehow. . . . My imagination blazed. The sensations the story aroused in me were never to leave me. (p. 47)

This is a most crucial passage in the narrative, for it gives us the first real indication of the boy's interest in imaginative literature. Moreover, the violence which lay at the heart of the story mirrored the violence in his own life and gave it a deeper meaning:

> I hungered for the sharp, frightening, breath-taking, almost painful excitement that the story had given me, and I vowed that as soon as I was old enough I would buy all the novels there were and read them to feed that thirst for violence that was in me, for intrigue, for plotting, for secrecy, for bloody murders. . . . They could not have known that Ella's whispered story of deception and murder had been the first experience in my life that had elicited from me a total emotional response. (p. 48)

He soon was to see the bloody drama of Bluebeard acted out in real life. While visiting his Aunt Maggie, Richard learns that Uncle Hoskins has been killed by whites who had long coveted his flourishing liquor business. On another occasion Matthews, Aunt Maggie's new husband, bludgeons the white girl who witnessed him stealing some money from her house and then sets the house on fire, leaving the girl to perish in the flames. There is also the violence which resulted at the close of the First World War when racial conflict permeated the South. The narrator recalls, "Though I did not witness any of it, I could not have been more thoroughly affected by it if I had participated directly in the clash" (p. 83).

The violence, the fear, the hunger—the basic realities of this boy's childhood—seemed to be symbolized in his mother's suffering, to the extent that, as he says, "her life set the emotional tone of my life." The suffering he experienced in his youth, he suggests, brought him to a deeper sense of communal responsibility:

> The spirit I had caught gave me insight into the sufferings of others, made me gravitate toward those whose feelings were like my own, made me sit for hours while others told me of their lives, made me strangely tender and cruel, violent and peaceful. (p. 112)

The entire passage here is clearly informed by a wider knowledge and consciousness than that of a twelve-year-old boy. The mature writer temporarily enters his narrative in order to interpret the experiences thus far recorded and to show their relevance to his general growth and development. By reflecting on his past in such a manner, he discovers himself in the present and justifies his present conduct and ideology in those past experiences.

When his mother's deteriorating health makes it necessary that he find some kind of employment, he has to confront the hatred and fear which he has seen debase and even destroy other blacks. So as the narrator moves from the relatively safe confines of his home and the black community into the white world, he appears as apprehensive about this venture as a Bigger Thomas entering the household of the Daltons: Bigger wonders, "Would they expect him to come in the front way or the back?" And, similarly, Richard wonders if his experiences at home and in his community have adequately prepared him for the hazards of the white world: "What would happen now that I would be among white people for hours at a stretch? Would they hit me? Curse me?"

At his first job, where he was to earn just two dollars a week, the white woman engages him in a significant dialogue:

"Now, boy, I want to ask you one question and I want you to tell me the truth," she said.

"Yes, ma'am," I said, all attention.

"Do you steal?" she asked seriously.

I bust into a laugh, then checked myself.

"What's so damn funny about that?" she asked.

"Lady, if I was a thief, I'd never tell anybody."

"What do you mean?" she blazed with a red face.

I had made a mistake during my first five minutes in the white world. I hung my head. (p. 160)

The two characters here are acting out a typical scene between blacks and whites in the South. But it is clearly a little drama in which the two parties are both to be viewed as victims of the southern caste system—the one because she has been trained only to echo conventional clichés about blacks, the other because, while conscious of the woman's ignorance, he must learn to disguise his true feelings, to dissemble and deny his own worth and dignity. For Richard, however, this feigning in the presence of whites proves to be an art most difficult to master. Even the counsel of his friend Griggs is of little help: "When you're in front of white people, think before you act, think before you speak. Your way of doing things is all right among our people, but not for white people. They won't stand for it" (p. 203). Griggs explains his own situation thus: "You know, Dick, you may think I'm an Uncle Tom, but I'm not. I hate these white people, hate 'em with all my heart. But I can't show it; if I did, they'd kill me" (p. 204). And though Richard can never be as submissive as the other black boys, he too would soon learn that, in the South, "acting" is often the only weapon of survival. "The safety of my life," he tells us later on in his account, "depended on how well I concealed from all whites what I felt" (p. 253).[10]

As he moves about from one job to the next, he slowly learns how a black boy is required to reckon with Jim Crow. At one job the woman is surprised that he, a black boy from Mississippi, does not know how to milk a cow; at another he is bitten by a dog only to be told by the foreman that he has "never seen a dog yet that could hurt a nigger"; at still another, he has what is nearly a violent confrontation with two white employees who are infuriated by his eagerness to learn a "white man's trade." Perhaps his most galling experience occurs while working as a hallboy in the Jackson hotel where, earlier, Ned's brother had been killed. While walking toward his home with one of the black maids headed in the same general direction, he becomes spellbound at seeing a white night watchman playfully slap her on the buttocks, but becomes even more astonished at the casualness with which the girl herself seems to treat the matter. He learns later that his brief moment of shock over such a routine act had almost cost him his life. Later, as a bellboy in the same hotel, he has to learn to avert his eyes from the white prostitutes who regularly lie nude across their beds. Reflecting on this, he writes: "Our presence awoke in them no sense of shame whatever, for we blacks were not considered human anyway" (p. 221).

In all of these experiences, Richard notes a concerted effort on the part of whites—given tacit approval by the blacks themselves—to consign him to a subservient role and to deny him that freedom of the will apart from which the creative mind cannot develop and flourish. In this context, the exchange with his first white employer takes on added significance. When the woman asks Richard why he is in school, the boy promptly responds that he wants to be a writer:

> "A what?" she demanded.
> "A writer," I mumbled.
> "For what?"
> "To write stories," I mumbled defensively.
> "You'll never be a writer," she said. "Who on earth put such ideas in your nigger head?" (p. 162)

Richard declares here what we have suspected all along, that he is interested in a literary career. The disclosure itself is not surprising, but the manner and circumstance under which it is made have significant implications. The woman was merely voicing a sentiment held by the majority of whites in the South: that there were certain areas of human endeavor beyond the range of possibility for any blacks. More tragic still, his own family and members of the black community seemed to have conspired with the white world in its effort to smother any capacity he might have for a literary career. Granny did not want Ella to read him her stories because they were "the devil's works." His own story, "The Voodoo of Hell's Half-Acre," only served further to alienate him from his schoolmates and family: "From no quarter, with the exception of the Negro newspaper editor, had there come a single encouraging word" (p. 186).

From this point on in the narrative the restrictions which Richard faces are those associated with his quest to become a writer. He dreams of going to the North, which is for him a place of freedom where he might, in his words, "do something to redeem my being alive." In so thinking, the narrator tells us:

> I was building up in me a dream which the entire educational system of the South had been rigged to stifle. I was feeling the very thing the state of Mississippi had spent millions of dollars to make sure I would never feel. . . . I was in my fifteenth year; in terms of schooling I was far behind the average youth of the nation, but I did not know that. In me was shaping a yearning for a kind of consciousness, a mode of being that the way of life about me had said could not be, must not be, and upon which the penalty of death had been placed. (pp. 186–87)

By way of stealing goods and reselling them—an act which, where any black person was concerned, was morally acceptable to the South—he finally acquires enough money to leave for Memphis. Although his experience in Memphis is no happier, at least here he is able to satisfy his childhood hunger for reading by devising a scheme for getting books from the public library—which is generally off limits to any blacks. Whites had often sent him to the library to get books for themselves. So he wonders how he might get books on his own. Having persuaded one of the more liberal whites to lend him his card, he forges the note:

"Let this nigger boy have some books by H. L. Mencken." In this manner, he is able to read a body of literature ranging all the way from Anatole France to Sinclair Lewis. What interests Richard most about the writers he encounters in this way is their ability to use language as a weapon for striking out against the ills plaguing society. These writers were, in the boy's mind, "fighting with words." "I derived from these novels," he says, "nothing less than a sense of life itself. All my life had shaped me for the realism, the naturalism of the modern novel, and I could not read enough of them" (p. 273). He says further: "It had been my accidental reading of fiction and literary criticism that had evoked in me a glimpse of life's possibilities" (p. 283).

The language of this entire concluding section of *Black Boy* is not that of the boy but that of the mature man, not that of the aspiring writer but that of the accomplished author. As the narrative ends before Richard's nineteenth year, the author, for the sake of his readers, has to furnish such information as will enable us to see the relationship between the experiences of the boy and the writer he finally became. But it is, in fact, a difficult connection for us to make, since Wright himself at the time had no clear conception of his future lifework. His random reading, impressive in its range as it was for a boy in his circumstances, afforded him no clear vision of the possibility of his electing a literary vocation. Indeed, it was only after he had become sufficiently removed from the galling experiences of his boyhood and had gained some understanding of the writer's craft that he could impose some pattern on the raw experiences of his past and transmute them into literary art. In this respect, then, *Black Boy* clearly points to *American Hunger*, which details his struggles to become a writer in Chicago. The book, which appeared in 1977, was originally designed to be published along with *Black Boy* as a single work. But at the behest of his publisher, Wright agreed to have the section treating his experiences in the North issued later as a separate volume, for both men realized that though this work offered important insights into Wright's later years, it had neither the scope nor the intensity of the volume which chronicled his years in the South.

So *Black Boy* stands as Wright's major achievement in the mode of autobiographical literature, and it presents the important events comprising his apprenticeship to life and to art. The violence, the fear, the hunger, and all such negative experiences would in time provide him with rich resources for his art, for "wringing meaning out of meaningless suffering."

Wright knew well that the way of the literary imagination—by which he was able eventually to deliver himself from the horrid experiences of his youth—was not an avenue open to the majority of blacks in the South. And though he failed to propose any concrete solutions to the dilemmas facing his people, his own story is an attempt to achieve a closer identification with those southern blacks who, like himself, had suffered under the heavy weight of racism but who, unlike Wright, lacked the talent to express in language the agony of their daily existence. In *American Hunger*, Wright observes: "I sensed that Negro life was a sprawling land of unconscious suffering and there were but a few Negroes who knew the meaning of their lives, who could tell their own stories."[11] His autobiography, then, is meant to be a "voice" for those "voiceless" blacks of his generation. The narrative strategy of the book functions at once to detail Wright's own effort to transcend the "bleakness" of black life in the South and to provide inspiration to the numerous other native sons and daughters who "had never been allowed to catch the full spirit of Western civilization." Ralph Ellison is correct in pointing out that Wright, in *Black Boy*, "has used his own life to probe what qualities of will, imagination and intellect are required of a Southern Negro to possess the meaning of his life in the United States."[12]

But, just as importantly, Wright wants to force the stewards of the southern caste system to take full responsibility for the many violations of human rights that blacks experienced. So he presents his case through the consciousness of a boy who does not understand why things are as they are. However, in his bewilderment and naiveté, the boy forces both blacks and whites to examine long-held practices and customs that retard relations in the South.

This autobiography, which takes the form of the *Bildungsroman*, does depict a boy's growth in consciousness but, in so doing, seeks to arouse the reader's consciousness as well. Wright knew well, of course, that those responsible for inflicting crimes upon blacks in the South were not likely to be moved to correct their abuses unless they could somehow be forced to see themselves not only as the perpetrators of those crimes but as their victims as well. In *Black Boy* and in Wright's other works, blacks commit acts of violence against whites, not necessarily out of any sense of vengeance but, rather, out of desperation and fear. Thus, Wright launches what amounts to a double-barreled attack upon racial brutality in the South. The white southerners who would not be aroused by his portrayal of a boy's difficult journey would surely be stirred when their own safety appeared to be at stake.

Wright's sense of community, however, did not make him blind to the shortcomings of his own people. In *Black Boy* he is critical of those blacks who passively accept the inferior roles assigned to them by the stewards of the southern caste system. He is keenly aware that "wearing the mask," even when such action appears expedient, means a sacrifice of one's dignity and self-respect. He laments, moreover, the fact that the blacks about him seem to be cut off from the spirit of Western culture, that they live in the "area of No Man's Land." But at the moment when Wright seems to be most convinced of the "barrenness of black life," one recognizes his own indebtedness to his folk tradition for his most essential subject matter and for the tones, images, and rhythms that constitute his style. For though he recognized the provinciality of southern black life, he also realized that here, in the very heart of the southern darkness, must be the starting point of his own quest for selfhood.

Notes

1. Cited by Guion Griffin Johnson, "Southern Paternalism toward Negroes after Emancipation," *Journal of Southern History* 23 (November 1957): 483–509.

2. See Richard Wright, *White Man, Listen!* (New York: Doubleday, 1957).

3. Morris Dickstein has also noted Wright's indebtedness to the *Bildungsroman* tradition, but it is a matter which he never develops in any detail. He states: "Wright's books, especially *Black Boy*, enunciate a fun-

damental pattern of black writing, that of the *Bildungsroman*, or, How I got my consciousness raised." See Robert Farnsworth and David Ray, eds., *Richard Wright: Impressions and Perspectives* (Ann Arbor: University of Michigan Press, 1971), p. 188.

4. Roy Pascal, *The German Novel* (Manchester, England: Manchester University Press, 1956), p. 11.

5. Michel Fabre speaks of the probability of Joyce's *Portrait* having influenced Wright's *Black Boy*, and he points out several parallels between the two works: "The power and sincerity of *Black Boy* had few predecessors, and the quality of the writing made it a new *Portrait of the Artist as a Young Man*. The influence of Joyce may not have been obvious, but the parallel immediately noted between his concerns and those of Wright was justified by many common features in their works: The protagonist's realization of belonging to a minority, the horror of a religion haunted by sex, and the difficulty of escaping from it." See Michel Fabre, *The Unfinished Quest of Richard Wright*, trans. Isabel Barzun (New York: Morrow, 1973), p. 253.

6. "How Richard Wright Looks at *Black Boy*," *PM Magazine*, April 14, 1945, p. 3.

7. Constance Webb, *Richard Wright: A Biography* (New York: Putnam's 1968), p. 203.

8. See Wayne C. Booth, *The Rhetoric of Fiction* (Chicago, Ill.: University of Chicago Press, 1961).

9. Richard Wright, *Black Boy* (1945; reprint, New York: Harper, 1966), p. 9. All subsequent citations from *Black Boy* are taken from this edition and will be cited in the text.

10. Richard Wright has made the following comment on the behavioral pattern known as "acting": "The American Negro's adversary is next door to him, on the street, in the job, in the school; hence acting has become almost a second nature with him. This acting regulates the manner, the tone of voice, even, in which most American Negroes speak to white men. The Negro's voice is almost always pitched high when addressed to a white man; all hint of aggressiveness is purged from it. In some instances an educated Negro will try to act as uneducated as possible in order not to merit rebuff from whites" (Wright, *White Man, Listen!* p. 43).

11. Richard Wright, *American Hunger* (New York: Harper, 1977), p. 7.

12. Ralph Ellison, *Shadow and Act* (New York: Random House, 1964), p. 77.

Creation of the Self in
Richard Wright's *Black Boy*

YOSHINOBU HAKUTANI

◆　◆　◆

I

*B*LACK BOY is generally acclaimed not only as the finest
autobiography written by a black author but as one of the
greatest autobiographies ever written in America. Critics, however, are not in agreement on what kind of autobiography it is.
W. E. B. Du Bois, for instance, wondered about the authenticity
of the book, saying, "The [sub]title, 'A Record of Childhood and
Youth,' makes one at first think that the story is autobiographical.
It probably is, at least in part. But mainly it is probably intended
to be fiction or fictionalized biography. At any rate the reader
must regard it as creative writing rather than simply a record of
life."[1] Yet even if one regards the book as a creative work rather
than an actual record of life, and despite its felicities of language,
Black Boy, Du Bois felt, falls short of its possible effectiveness because it is "so patently and terribly overdrawn."[2] Those who are
not impressed by the book criticize the excessive emphasis on
violence, meanness, and despair in Wright's work. Moreover, they
are not convinced of the authenticity of *Black Boy* as an autobiography because they feel that the world, bad as it is, cannot be
so bad as Wright says it is.

Even those who are convinced of its authenticity do not necessarily consider it a higher accomplishment than *Native Son*. When
the book appeared, many distinguished writers became its advo-
cates: Sinclair Lewis, William Faulkner, Gertrude Stein, Henry Miller, Ralph Ellison, Lionel Trilling. Among them, Faulkner, who
perhaps knew black life in the South as well as anyone, wrote to

Wright that he was deeply moved by *Black Boy*, but commented that what is said in it is better said in *Native Son*. "The good lasting stuff," Faulkner wrote, "comes out of one individual's imagination and sensitivity to and comprehension of the sufferings of Everyman, Anyman, not out of the memory of his own grief."[3] This response by a fellow novelist suggests that *Black Boy* suffers as a work of art since Wright's method here is less impersonal than it is in a novel like *Native Son*. To Faulkner, art cannot be created when too much is made of one's own life; dealing with impersonal forces of nature and society in such a novel as *Native Son* requires a sense of detachment. For this reason Faulkner said, "I hope you will keep on saying it, but I hope you will say it as an artist, as in *Native Son*."[4]

Faulkner's evaluation is based on the assumption that *Black Boy* is an autobiography. But the narrator of the book takes such an impersonal attitude that the book as a whole may not sound like a usual autobiography. As Du Bois has noted, there is a genuine paucity of personal love or affection expressed toward Wright's mother in *Black Boy*.[5] The young Wright amply expresses his awe and wonder at his suffering mother. He is unable to understand the reason that she was deserted by her husband, broken by paralysis, and overwhelmed by every unimaginable circumstance she had to face. His reaction, as a narrator, is intellectual rather than personal. By contrast, in Theodore Dreiser's autobiography of his youth, *Dawn*, the narrator's wonder at his equally suffering mother is tinged with personal sorrow and sympathy. In short, Wright's intention in *Black Boy* seems to have been to portray his experience with naturalistic objectivity, rather than from a personal point of view.

A literary naturalist is expected to establish a milieu taken from life and, into it, project characters who then act in accordance with that milieu. The naturalist must record, without comment or interpretation, what actually happens. If Wright regarded himself as a fictional persona in *Black Boy*, he would be less concerned with either his own life or his own point of view. The focus of his interest in the book would be on the events that occurred

outside of his life. It is understandable, then, that Wright's account of his own life would not be entirely authentic. One might
even suspect that Wright's self-portrait would abound with fictional accounts, and, indeed, many differences between *Black Boy*
and his life have been pointed out. One reviewer's objection to
the book as autobiography is based on discrepancies found between Wright's accounts in the book and "The Ethics of Living
Jim Crow."[6] For example, *Black Boy* describes a fight between
Wright and a group of white boys in which he was injured behind
the ear and later ushered to a doctor by his mother, whereas in
his "Ethics of Living Jim Crow," Wright relates that "a kind neighbor saw me and rushed me to a doctor, who took three stitches
in my neck." Also in *Black Boy* Wright often refers to his mother
as a cook "in the white folks' kitchen" and describes her as less
intellectual than she really was.[7] In fact, Ella Wilson, his mother,
before her marriage to his father, was well educated for a black
woman and taught school. Edwin R. Embree, who intimately
knew Wright's youth and early literary career, testifies that "his
mother, light brown, good looking, possessed of a few years of
book learning, got jobs a few months as a teacher at $25.00 a
month."[8]

These alterations, however, are not a major reason for calling
Black Boy a fictionalized biography. Even though parts of the book
are fictional, it is nervertheless autobiographical and should not
be equated with a novel. No one for a moment can overlook the
fact that it portrays Wright himself, and if it concerns others,
their lives are necessarily intertwined with his. But the most important distinction *Black Boy* bears as autobiography is Wright's
intention to use the young self as a mask. The attitudes and
sentiments expressed by the young Wright are not totally his own
but represent the responses of those he called "the voiceless Negro
boys" of the South.[9] Such a technique makes *Black Boy* a unique
autobiography just as a similar technique makes *Native Son* a
unique novel. (Wright tells us that Bigger Thomas is a conscious
composite portrait of numerous individual blacks he has known
in his life.)[10]

II

The uniqueness of Wright's autobiography can be explained in another way. Since he is a spokesman for the voiceless black youths of the South he had known in his life, he must be objective and scientific in his observations. Thus *Black Boy*, though not intended as such, is a convincing sociological study. Like sociology, it not only analyzes a social problem but offers a solution to the problem it treats. Wright's purpose is to study the way in which black life in the South was determined by its environment, and, to borrow Émile Zola's words, his desire is to "disengage the determinism of human and social phenomena so that we may one day control and direct these phenomena."[11] Wright is constantly trying to make his investigation systematic and unbiased. He is concerned with the specific social forces in the environment of a black boy: white racism, black society, and his own family.

James Baldwin has accused Wright of believing that "in Negro life there exists no tradition, no field of manners, no possibility of ritual or intercourse, such as may, for example, sustain the Jew even after he has left his father's house."[12] Unlike Baldwin, who grew up in a highly religious black community in Harlem, Wright in the deep South witnessed "the essential bleakness of black life in America" (p. 33). The central issue, however, is whether such human traits as, in Wright's words, "tenderness, love, honor, loyalty, and the capacity to remember" are innate in the Negro tradition, as Baldwin says, or are "fostered, won, struggled and suffered for," as Wright believed (p. 33). Elsewhere Wright tells us that he "wrote the book to tell a series of incidents strung through my childhood, but the main desire was to render a judgment on my environment. . . . That judgment was this: the environment the South creates is too small to nourish human beings, especially Negro human beings."[13] Wright, therefore, squarely places the burden of proof on white society, contending with enough justification given in *Black Boy* that the absence of these human qualities in black people stemmed from years of white oppression.

To Wright, the effect of white oppression in the South was most visible in the black communities of the Mississippi Delta. By the time he became fourteen he was able to read and write well enough to obtain a job, in which he assisted an illiterate black insurance salesman. On his daily rounds to the shacks and plantations in the area, he was appalled by the pervasiveness of segregated life: "I saw a bare, bleak pool of black life and I hated it; the people were alike, their homes were alike, and their farms were alike" (p. 120). Such observations later infuriated not only white segregationists but many black citizens, who wrote letters to the FBI and denounced *Black Boy*. Letters called him "a black Nazi" and "one of the biggest spreaders of race hatred." Another black protester complained: "I am an American Negro and proud of it because we colored people in America have come a long way in the last seventy years . . . We colored people don[']t mind the truth but we do hate lies or anything that disturb[s] our peace of mind."[14]

What had, at first, disturbed Wright was not the failure of many blacks and whites alike to see the facts of racism, but their inability to recognize malice in the minds of white racists. *Black Boy* recounts an incident in which Wright was once wrongfully accused of addressing a white employee at an optical company without using the title "Mr." Another white employee later corroborated the accusation by telling Wright: "Didn't you call him *Pease*? If you say you didn't, I'll rip your gut string loose with this f–k–g bar, you black granny dodger! You can't call a white man a liar and get away with it!" (p. 166). Consequently Wright was forced to leave his job. Resenting a black man obtaining what they considered a white man's occupation, these white men deliberately created a falsehood to deny Wright a livelihood.

In retrospect, however, Wright realizes that such grudges as white men held against black men did not seem to derive from the white men themselves. He theorizes that they were not acting as individual men, but as "part of a huge, implacable, elemental design toward which hate was futile" (p. 170). Wright's autobiography does not for one moment concern itself with the theme of evil, as romantic fiction or tragic drama sometimes does.[15] *Black*

Boy is intended as a sociological document rather than a novel; what such a document shows is the fact that the oppressors are as much victims of the elemental design of racism as are the oppressed. The center of Wright's interest, then, rests on deciphering this design.

In *Black Boy* Wright is continually at pains to show that white people have a preconceived notion of a Negro's place in the South: He serves them, he is likely to steal, and he cannot read or write. The taboo subjects that southerners refused to discuss with black men included "American white women; the Ku Klux Klan; France, and how Negro soldiers fared while there; Frenchwomen; Jack Johnson; the entire northern part of the United States; the Civil War; Abraham Lincoln; U.S. Grant; General Sherman; Catholics; the Pope; Jews; the Republican Party; slavery; social equality; Communism; Socialism; the 13th, 14th, and 15th Amendments of the Constitution" (p. 202). Sex and religion were the most accepted subjects, for they were the topics that did not require positive knowledge or self-assertion on the part of the black man. White men did not mind black men talking about sex as long as it was not interracial. Sex was considered purely biological, and like religion it would not call for the will power of an individual. Although blacks were physically free, the South had replaced traditional slavery with a system by which their freedom of speech and movement was closely monitored and restricted. The culprit was not any individual white man; it was the complicity of white society that had allowed the design of slavery to renew itself in the twentieth-century South.

What underlies this new design of slavery? Most significantly, black men are classified as animals, a mentality inherited from the old days of slavery. Not only are black people considered to be white men's servants, but they are expected to entertain them as though blacks were animals in the zoo. Crimes perpetrated on fellow blacks are not condemned as such. Wright cites an incident in which his foreman at a company he worked for instigated antagonism between Wright and a black employee at another company so that they would try to stab each other. Wright, avoiding the trap, agreed instead to fight a boxing match to satisfy the white employees' whim. "I suppose," Wright reasoned, "it's fun for white men to see niggers fight. . . . To white men we're like dogs or cocks" (pp. 207–8). Even killing among black men would not prick the white men's consciences. Such an attitude echoes that of the white public at the trial of Bigger Thomas for the murder of Bessie Mears, his black girlfriend, in *Native Son.*

Another degrading assumption white men hold about black men is that, since they are treated as animals, they are not supposed to possess intellectual capabilities. The reason for the young Wright losing employment is often related to his intelligence, which poses a threat to the white man's sense of superiority. Wright points out, for instance, that some black men tried to organize themselves and petitioned their white employers for higher wages and better working conditions. But he correctly observes that such a movement was swiftly avenged by further restrictions and brutality. Throughout the book Wright continues to demonstrate the fact that southern whites would rather have blacks who stole goods and property than blacks who were conscious, however vaguely, of the worth of their own intelligence and humanity. For Wright, racism induces black deceit and encourages black irresponsibility. Ironically, blacks are rewarded to the degree that they can make the whites feel safe and allow them to maintain their moral superiority.

Needless to say, the forces of racism have devastating effects on black life. Critics, both black and white, have complained that Wright in *Black Boy* lacks racial pride. It is true that he is critical of the black community in the South, but it is not true that he places the blame on the black community itself. His intention is to show that a racist system produced the way of life that was forced on black people. In terms of social determinism, *Black Boy* provides a literary experiment to demonstrate uniformity in Negro behavior under the influence of social forces.[16]

Most black people, he admits, do adjust to their environment for survival. But in doing so they lose individuality, self-respect, and dignity. This is perhaps the reason that Benjamin Davis, Jr., a black leftist critic, attacked Wright's portrayal of the southern black community: "*Black Boy* says some wholly unacceptable

adjust-ment = dimish-ment

It is racism that narrows + constricts Black Life —

things about the Negro's capacity for genuine emotion."[17] To Wright, however, it is the circumstances in which Negroes find themselves that cause the personalities to warp, and this in turn results in various forms of hypocritical and erratic behavior. The most striking example of this appears in an incident with an elevator boy whom the young Wright encountered in Memphis. The black boy, who professed that "he was proud of his race and indignant about its wrongs," never hesitated to expose his buttocks for a white man to kick so he could solicit a quarter from the white man. Wright tells us he felt "no anger or hatred, only disgust and loathing," and that he confronted this youth:

> "How in God's name can you do that?"
> "I needed a quarter and I got it," he said soberly, proudly.
> "But a quarter can't pay you for what he did to you," I said.
> "Listen, nigger," He said to me, "my ass is tough and quarters is scarce." (p. 200)

About white men's sexual exploitation of black women, Wright is as much critical of black women as of white men, because black women expect and readily condone white men's behavior. Once, a black maid who had been slapped playfully on her buttocks by a white night watchman told the indignant Wright who had witnessed the incident: " 'They never get any further with us than that, if we don't want 'em to' " (p. 174).

Understandably such portraits of black men and women made some readers feel that Wright unduly deprived black people of their personal honor and dignity. For Ralph Ellison, Wright's autobiography lacks "high humanity," especially among its blacks. As Dan McCall correctly argues, however, "Wright is trying to show us how this gross state came about. He refuses to dress up his Negroes in an imported Sunday best because he has a far larger task before him."[18] Wright explains:

> I began to marvel at how smoothly the black boys acted out the roles that the white race had mapped out for them. Most

of them were not conscious of living a special, separated, stunted way of life. Yet I knew that in some period of their growing up—a period that they had no doubt forgotten— there had been developed in them a delicate, sensitive controlling mechanism that shut off their mind and emotions from all that the white race had said was taboo. (p. 172)

One of the remarkable insights *Black Boy* offers is that social determinism takes its heaviest toll in Wright's family life. One would assume that if black boys are mistreated in society at large, they would at least be protected in their family. But in Wright's early childhood his father deserted his wife and children; not only did Wright become a casualty of the broken family, but his father himself was a victim of the racial system in the deep South. Wright observes about his father: "From the white landowners above him there had not been handed to him a chance to learn the meaning of loyalty, of sentiment, of tradition" (p. 30).

Consequently, the young Wright was subjected to the crushing blow of family antagonisms.[19] His grandmother's Seventh Day Adventist doctrine as practiced at home epitomized this hostility and strife. Wright saw "more violent quarrels in our deeply religious home than in the home of a gangster, burglar, or a prostitute. . . . The naked will to power seemed always to walk in the wake of a hymn" (p. 119). While Granny held on to the helm of the family, several of Wright's uncles also attempted to administer their authority. One of them, enraged by Wright's impolite mannerisms, scolded his nephew for not acting as "the backward black boys act on the plantations"; he was ordered "to grin, hang my head, and mumble apologetically when I was spoken to" (p. 138). It seems as though black adults, subjected to racism in white society, in turn felt compelled to rule their children at home. The black adults had grown up in a world in which they were permitted no missteps in a white-dominated society. The fact that Wright's worst punishments, such as those given by his mother for setting fire to his grandmother's house, were inflicted by his closest relatives suggests how completely black life was dominated by white racism.

no man's land

stereotype of acceptance

III

Despite the naturalistic philosophy that underlies Wright's vision of black life, the miracle of *Black Boy* is that its hero, by the time he left for Chicago, had not become the patient, humorous, subservient black man of the white myth. Nor did he end up as either the degraded, grinning, and perpetually frustrated Negro or as a murderer like Bigger Thomas of *Native Son*. Throughout the book Wright is at great pains to create a manhood as a direct challenge to the overwhelming forces of society. *Black Boy* reveals how self-creation can be thwarted and mauled, but unlike James Farrell's *Studs Lonigan* or Dreiser's *An American Tragedy*, the hero's spirit remains unbroken. Most important, however, what distinguishes *Black Boy* from any other naturalistic work is that it is the story of a man estranged from his own race by sensitivity and intellect, yet segregated from the white race by the color of his skin.

doubly segregated

Finding himself in no-man's-land, the young Wright attempted to create his own world. Although *Black Boy* is predominantly a portrayal of southern society, it is also a self-portrait. Despite the devastating effects of the society on his own life, he came to the conclusion that anything was "possible, likely, feasible, because I wanted everything to be possible" (p. 64). Early in the book he rationalizes this passion for ego: "Because I had no power to make things happen outside of me in the objective world, I made things happen within. Because my environment was bare and bleak, I endowed it with unlimited potentialities, redeemed it for the sake of my own hungry and cloudy yearning" (p. 64).

About this process of self-creation, critics have charged that he deliberately degrades black life to dramatize the emergence of the self as a hero.[20] But given his life as we know it today, one can scarcely deny the authenticity of the events recounted in the book, nor are the episodes about racism unbelievable or unconvincing. Although Du Bois argues that "the suffering of others is put down simply as a measure of his own suffering and resentment,"[21] it is understandable that Wright did so in order to make his own life representative of the voiceless black boys, as well as to indicate that they too are capable of self-creation.

Whether or not our hero is too selfish and proud an achiever to be credible can be judged by how convincingly his maturation is portrayed. In his early childhood Wright acquired a hatred for white people, not based on his own experience, but derived from other Negro children. Like any child, black or white, Wright had his vision circumscribed by blinders and colored glasses. As he grew older, however, he realized that the roots of racial hatred did not exist in any individuals, but stemmed from an inherited system. The white race was as much its victim as the black race. From this vantage point, he took social determinism to be a threat to his autonomy and began to wage a battle. By the time he was nineteen, he became aware that his life experiences "had shaped me to live by my own feelings and thoughts" (p. 221).

It was the crushing effect of environment and temperament that Wright learned so well from his immediate relatives. When he was a young boy, one of his uncles was murdered by his white business competitors; his grandmother was a religious fanatic. The greatest blow to his childhood came from his own father, who succumbed to the temptation of sex and alcohol. When he saw his father again a quarter of a century later, he realized that, "though ties of blood made us kin, though I could see a shadow of my face in his face, though there was an echo of my voice in his voice, we were forever strangers, speaking a different language, living on vastly distant planes of reality" (p. 30). Not only is Wright denying the influence of heredity on his own character, but he is distinguishing two men subjected to the same environment. His father, Wright concluded, "was a black peasant who had gone to the city seeking life, but . . . whose life had been hopelessly snarled in the city, and who had at last fled the city— that same city which had lifted me in its burning arms and borne me toward alien and undreamed-of shores of knowing" (p. 31).

What, then, were the forces in his life that young Wright had learned to ward off in his struggle for independence? Throughout his youth he witnessed how deeply superstitious religion had trapped the minds and hearts of black people. As a child he was

The parting of father + sons

impressed with the elders at church for the inspiring language of their sermons: "a gospel clogged with images of vast lakes of eternal fire, of seas vanishing, of valleys of dry bones, ... of the lame walking; a salvation that teemed with fantastic beasts having multiple heads and horns and eyes and feet" (p. 89). But such sensations departed quickly once he left the church and saw the bright sunshine with the crowded people pouring into the streets. To him none of these religious ideas and images seemed to have anything to do with his life. He knew not only that religion had a capacity to mesmerize people in the black community, but also that it was used by "one individual or group to rule another in the name of God" (p. 119).

As some critics have noted, *Black Boy* is relatively free from the hero's references to his own sexual awakening.[22] Sex in *Black Boy* is treated much like religion, for Wright knew during his adolescent years that one could be easily victimized by sexual forces. The only time sexual attraction is mentioned is in connection with a church service in which Wright, at twelve, was infatuated with the elder's wife. The fact that the woman is depicted in grotesquely physical terms rather than spiritual and felicitous images ("a black imp with two horns; ... a scaly, naked body; wet, sticky fingers; moist, sensual lips; and lascivious eyes") suggests that he is indeed debasing his sexual attraction (p. 98). That he could easily fend off such biological forces can be contrasted with Fishbelly Tucker's unsuccessful struggle with his sexual problems in *The Long Dream*. In that novel, sex is dealt with in its sordid context; the hero's ritual of initiation into manhood is performed in a house of prostitution.

Although *Black Boy* is strung with a series of episodes that illustrates various forms of racial oppression, the center of attention lies in our hero's transcendence of that oppression. Racial oppression is caused not only by the external forces of society but by the internal problems of the oppressed. "Some," Wright admits, "may escape the general plight and grow up, but it is a matter of luck."[23] To the hero of *Black Boy*, most of them were victims of racial prejudice, failures in the battle for survival. No small wonder an anonymous reviewer, calling *Black Boy* "the most

ferocious exercise in misanthropy since Jonathan Swift," was appalled by the hatred Wright expresses toward both whites and
blacks.[24] Obviously, the reader misunderstood Wright's intention,
for the book is not meant to be a satire like *Gulliver's Travels*, in
which the narrator assails and loathes every conceivable human
vice and depravity. Rather, *Black Boy* is Wright's honest attempt
to refute a naturalistic philosophy of life. Our hero is a catalyst
in accomplishing this task.

In "Blueprint for Negro Writing," Wright asserts that "theme
for Negro writers will rise from understanding the meaning of
their being transplanted from a 'savage' to a 'civilized' culture in
all its social, political, economic, and emotional implications."[25]
In *Black Boy*, his chief aim is to show how this youth, whom the
South called a "nigger," surmounted his obstacles in the civilized
culture. The most painful stance he took in this struggle was to
be an intense individualist; he created selfhood and exerted his
will at the risk of annihilation. In scene after scene both the black
and the white community kept piling crushing circumstances
upon him, but no matter how unbearably they were pressed
down on him, he refused to give in. Only under such pressure
can one discover one's self. For others, this process of creation
might have been aided by chance, but for him "it should be a
matter of plan." And himself an exemplar, Wright defined the
mission as "a matter of saving the citizens of our country for our
country."[26]

One could be puzzled by this youth's individuality and forti-
tude if the seed of manhood had not been sown in the child.
Despite a critic's disclaimer to the contrary, *Black Boy* contains
ample evidence for the child's precocity and independence.[27]
Wright's earlier self is presented even to the point of betraying
his vanity: When he moved to his grandmother's house after his
family was deserted by his father, he took pride in telling the
timid children of the new neighborhood about his train ride, his
cruise on the *Kate Adams* on the Mississippi River, and his escape
from the orphanage (p. 33). Moreover, the young child is presented as a rebel who refuses to compromise with the dictates of
society and family. Once he was dismayed to find out that the

man who had beaten a black boy was not the boy's father. Though Wright was told by his mother that he was "too young to understand," he responded with a resolution: "I'm not going to let anybody beat me" (p. 21). This youthful attitude gave rise to an even more awesome resolution, of which he later became capable when he heard the story of a black woman who had avenged her husband's murder. According to the rumor, when she was granted permission to claim her husband's body for burial, she took with her a shotgun wrapped in a white sheet and, while kneeling down before the white executioners, shot four of them—a tale that served as the exact prototype of "Bright and Morning Star." *Black Boy* records the young Wright's belligerency:

> I resolved that I would emulate the black woman if I were ever faced with a white mob; I would conceal a weapon, pretend that I had been crushed by the wrong done to one of my loved ones; then, just when they thought I had accepted their cruelty as the law of my life, I would let go with my gun and kill as many of them as possible before they killed me. The story of the woman's deception gave form and meaning to confused defensive feelings that had long been sleeping in me. (p. 65)

Becoming a rebel inevitably led to being a misfit. In Wright's life, however, it is his innate character that allowed this to happen. How self-assertive the young Wright was can be best demonstrated in a comparison between him and his playmates. Although he identified himself with a mistreated group, there was a crucial difference between him and other black children. They constantly complained about the petty wrongs they suffered, but they had no desire to question the larger issues of racial oppression. Their attitude resembles that of the young Fishbelly in *The Long Dream;* just like his father before him, Fishbelly servilely worships the powerful white people. He falls in love with the values of the white world because such demeanor can offer him material rewards and make his manhood easier and less painful to achieve.

The young Wright, on the other hand, found among the black boys no sympathy for his inquiring mind. As a result he was forced to contemplate such questions for himself.

As early as twelve years old, Wright held "a sense of the world that was mine and mine alone, a notion as to what life meant that no education could ever alter, a conviction that the meaning of living came only when one was struggling to wring a meaning out of meaningless suffering" (pp. 87–88). His decision to leave the South seven years later, the final action of our hero, was based upon such conviction, as if the seed of manhood had already been in the child. Without mental companionship to rely on, however, he withdrew and turned inward like the antihero of an existentialist novel. In his recoil he had once again discovered that the revelation of all truths must come through the action and anguish of the self. It was at this point in his ordeal that he came in contact with the works of American realists such as H. L. Mencken, Theodore Dreiser, and Sherwood Anderson. It was their ideas, he tells us, that literally delivered his brooding sensibility to a brighter horizon, a vision that "America could be shaped nearer to the hearts of those who lived in it" (p. 227). It was also at this time that he decided to head north to discover for himself that man could live with dignity and determine his own destiny. Because he knew he could not make the world, he sought to make things happen within him and caught a sense of freedom; in so doing he discovered the new world.

Notes

1. "Richard Wright Looks Back," *New York Herald Tribune*, 4 Mar. 1945, p. 2.
2. Ibid.
3. "Letter to Richard Wright," in *Richard Wright: Impressions and Perspectives*, ed. David Ray and Robert M. Farnsworth (Ann Arbor: University of Michigan Press, 1973), p. 143.
4. Ibid.
5. Du Bois, "Richard Wright Looks Back," p. 2.
6. See Beatrice M. Murphy, *Pulse* 3 (Apr. 1945): 32–33.

7. Richard Wright, *Black Boy: A Record of Childhood and Youth* (New York: Harper, 1945), p. 17. Later references are to this edition and indicated in parentheses.

8. See "Richard Wright: Native Son," in *Thirteen against the Odds*, ed. Edwin Rogers Embree (New York: Viking, 1944), pp. 25–26.

9. See Wright, "The Handiest Truth to Me to Plow Up Was in My Own Life," *P.M. Magazine*, 4 Apr. 1945, p. 3.

10. "How 'Bigger' Was Born," in *Native Son* (1940; reprint, New York: Harper & Row, 1966), p. xii.

11. "The Experimental Novel," in *Documents of Modern Literary Realism*, ed. George J. Becker (Princeton, NJ: Princeton University Press, 1963), p. 181.

12. *Notes of a Native Son* (1955, reprint, New York: Bantam, 1968), p. 28.

13. Wright, "The Handiest Truth," p. 3.

14. See Addison Gayle, *Richard Wright: Ordeal of a Native Son* (Garden City, NY: Anchor Press/Doubleday, 1980), pp. 173–74. According to Gayle, Senator Bilbo of Mississippi condemned *Black Boy* on the floor of the U.S. Senate on 7 June 1945 as "the dirtiest, filthiest, lousiest, most obscene piece of writing that I have ever seen in print. . . . it is so filthy and dirty. . . . it comes from a Negro, and you cannot expect any better from a person of his type" (p. 173).

15. In general I agree with Dan McCall, who says: "Wright knew that all the evil could not be laid to a man. He refused to create a 'white villain,' . . . In *Black Boy* we see no villains; we do not even see a series of villains. We see men utterly helpless; varieties of foulness, stunted minds" (*The Example of Richard Wright* [New York: Harcourt, 1969], p. 128).

16. Edward Margolies observes: "Wright traps the reader in a stereotyped response—the same stereotyped response that Wright is fighting throughout the book: that is, that all Negroes are alike and react alike" (*The Art of Richard Wright* [Carbondale: Southern Illinois University Press, 1969], p. 19).

17. "Some Impressions of *Black Boy*," *Daily Worker*, 1 Apr. 1945, p. 9.

18. McCall, *Example of Richard Wright*, pp. 118–19.

19. *Black Boy* as autobiography can be closely compared with Angelo Herndon's *Let Me Live* (1937). Both writers depict the forces of segregation that had devastating effects on their educations and job opportunities. Both describe poverty and hunger in the plights of their families. But, while Wright grew up without his father and with his bedridden mother

and hostile relatives, Herndon could rely on the traditional family loyalty—a father with trust and confidence in his son and a warm-hearted, loving mother.

20. W. E. B. Du Bois writes: "After this sordid, shadowy picture we gradually come upon the solution. The hero is interested in himself, is self-centered to the exclusion of everybody and everything else" ("Richard Wright Looks Back," p. 2). John M. Reilly also argues that Wright "will not risk telling experiences inconsistent in any way with his image of himself as an alienated peasant youth in rebellion against the hostile Southern caste system. . . . Wright suppresses his connections with the bourgeoisie. Had he mentioned these connections, Wright might have modified the picture of a bleak and hostile environment, but there is no question of falsification" ("Self-Portraits by Richard Wright," *Colorado Quarterly* 22 [Summer 1971]: 34).

21. Du Bois, "Richard Wright Looks Back," p. 2.

22. Edward Margolies considers sex in *Black Boy* in terms of "violence (the dangers inherent in relationships with white prostitutes); bravado (adolescent boys speaking of their prowess); adultery (his father's abandonment of his wife for another woman); obscenities (which Wright learned at the age of six); or condescension and rejection (Wright's fending off the daughter of his landlady in Memphis because she was incapable of understanding the depths of his sensibilities)" (*The Art of Richard Wright*, pp. 17–18). Katherine Fishburn maintains that *The Long Dream* has more detail and a much more thorough treatment of a young black's sexual maturation than *Black Boy* (*Richard Wright's Hero: The Faces of a Rebel-Victim* [Metuchen, NJ: Scarecrow, 1977], p. 14).

23. Wright, "The Handiest Truth," p. 3.

24. *Newark Evening News*, 17 Mar. 1945.

25. In *Richard Wright Reader*, ed. Ellen Wright and Michel Fabre (New York: Harper & Row, 1978), p. 47.

26. Wright, "The Handiest Truth," p. 3.

27. Reviewer F. K. Richter observed that *Black Boy* is an unconscious demonstration of Aristotle's entelechy, that manhood resides in childhood. But he maintains that because Wright fails to provide indispensable factors that made the child grow, "the book loses some of its value as autobiography and non-fiction and takes on, however slightly, a quality of fiction" (*Negro Story* 1 [May–June 1945]: 93–95).

"Shouting Curses"

The Politics of "Bad" Language in
Richard Wright's Black Boy

JENNIFER H. POULOS

◆　◆　◆

In "EVERYBODY'S PROTEST NOVEL," James Baldwin envisions Richard Wright and Harriet Beecher Stowe in mortal combat: "it seems that the contemporary Negro novelist and the dead New England woman are locked together in a deadly, time-less battle; the one uttering merciless exhortations, the other shouting curses."[1] Richard Wright's shouted curse is his novel *Native Son* (1940). In 1945, Richard Wright published *Black Boy*,[2] an autobiographical text in which he literally curses his way through the early part of his life. A concern with the nature and use of "bad" language[3] marks *Black Boy*. Wright's deployment of bad language plays a crucial role in shaping him as an African-American artist. For *Black Boy* considers not only the development of an artist but the conflict inherent in the very idea of becoming an African-American artist and of gaining control over a tool—lan-guage—which traditionally barred or curtailed African-American expression.

The importance of education, and of learning to read and write in particular, is a pronounced theme in African-American literature, dating at least from the time of the slave narrative. As Frederick Douglass explained the racial politics of education through the mouth of his master. " 'Learning would *spoil* the best nigger in the world. Now,' said he, 'if you teach that nigger . . . how to read, there would be no keeping him. It would forever unfit him to be a slave.' "[4] The ability to express oneself as an educated person can alter fundamentally the identity of a slave; the struggle for self-expression is the struggle for freedom.

Thus from slavery onward, the meaning of "bad" language doubles back on itself. "Bad" language can be good; the "obscenity" of an African American expressing herself also frees African Americans from the stereotypes imposed on them by an oppressive white culture. Such self-expression is also "bad" because it endangers the life of the African American who disrupts the racist status quo. These contradictions underlie the slang term "bad" in African-American culture. As Tony Thorne defines the term, "bad" means "good," and originates "from the terminology of the poorest black Americans, either as simple irony or based on the assumption that what is bad in the eyes of the white establishment is good for them."[5] An African American who speaks proper English may in fact court alienation from her own community. Zora Neale Hurston's experiences in Florida provide a striking illustration of this phenomenon:

> I went about asking, in carefully-accented Barnardese, "Pardon me, but do you know any folk-tales or folk-songs?" The men and women who had whole treasuries of material just seeping through their pores looked at me and shook their heads.[6]

The African-American community understands that language is not a simple communication tool and acts with full awareness of the political uses of labeling language "good" or "bad."

To compose *Black Boy*, Richard Wright negotiated through a language fully implicated in the hierarchies of social power. As Horace Porter notes, "Wright's incredible struggle to master words is inextricably bound to his defiant quest for individual existence and expression."[7] Wright needed language to express himself, but in acquiring these skills he risked becoming "bad" by definition of both African-American and white cultures. To become the artist he wanted to be, Richard Wright had to overcome the "badness" ascribed to his expression because he was African American and avoid complicity with Western ideas of "good literature." He needed to turn "bad" and "good" into "bad" in the African-American sense. Richard Wright accomplishes this negotiation in *Black Boy* by linking literal "bad" language—dirty words, obscenities, curses—with ideas of inappropriate speech as defined by a racist society. He plays these notions off each other to redefine notions of "good" and "bad" language.

As narrator, Wright does not use direct citations of swearing frequently in the text until the younger Richard has mastered their meaning and use. When Aunt Jody catches him swearing—"That goddam lousy bastard sonofabitching bucket!" (*BB* 113)—Richard is in control of the terms. He may shock his family, but his use of these terms is, in a sense, appropriate and justified because the water has spilled all over him. Earlier in the text, when Richard's use of profanity is inappropriate to events, Wright represses the actual words. He does not transcribe the remarks Richard repeated in the saloon or the text of his soap words. When Richard tells Granny to "kiss back there," Wright suppresses profanity with euphemism. Even the foul language of the saloon patrons is absent from the text. This strategy allows Wright to claim the "badness" of the language while retaining a "good" surface, thus foiling attempts to judge his prose as inferior or obscene.

Wright places indiscriminate, inappropriate swearing in the mouths of whites. When Wright narrates his early work experiences, he reprints in detail and at length the bad language of his employers. Whites swear gratuitously and with the intention of degrading others; these people are not the laughing saloon patrons:

> "What the hell!" he snarled. "Every morning it's these damn eggs for breakfast."
> "Listen, you sonofabitch," the woman said, sitting too, "you don't have to eat 'em."
> "You might try serving some dirt," he said, and forked up the bacon.
> I felt I was dreaming. Were they like that all the time? If

so, I would not stay here. A young girl came and flopped into her chair.

"That's right, you bitch," the young man said. "Knock the food right out of my goddamn mouth."

"You know what you can do," the girl said. (*BB* 175)

This dramatic and callous use of profanity is typical of whites and is completely inappropriate to the situation: breakfast. In a book in which a recurring theme is hunger, the young man's cavalier dismissal of a breakfast that Richard, understating the case, calls "promising" (*BB* 175) emphasizes the obscenity of the language by inflecting it through racism. Richard is chronically underfed because of poverty generated by segregation, while whites seem indifferent to the benefits they receive from the oppression of African Americans. Wright here couples Richard's first extended experience with racism with an upsurge of bad language in the text which undercuts stereotypical definitions of the domain of "bad" language.

Wright elaborates on this concept in Richard's experiences at the optician's shop in Jackson, Mississippi. Reynolds and Pease, white lens grinders, begin to abuse Richard when he tries to learn their trade, as he had been promised when he was hired. Once Richard moves out of his place as cleaning boy and errand runner, "they changed. . . . they said good morning no more. When I was just a bit slow in performing some duty, I was called a lazy black sonofabitch" (*BB* 222). Reynolds and Pease disparage black sexuality—"I heard that a nigger can stick his prick in the ground and spin around on it like a top. . . . I'd give you a dime, if you did it" (*BB* 222–23)—then terrorize him into quitting. They call him a "black sonofabitch," a "granny dodger," and talk about hitting him with a "f–k–g bar" (*BB* 224–25). Racism generates profanity. Wright, using excessive amounts of bad language here, retains for himself the ability to use bad language judiciously. At the level of the text, Richard Wright is in full control of bad language.

Within the text, however, Wright links episodes of inappropriate speech to literal "bad language" to explore the badness, by definition, of all attempts of African Americans at self-expression. The two horrific scenes which open *Black Boy*—the house fire and the hanging of the kitten—lay the groundwork for Richard Wright's determination to speak and the treachery this project involves. By their shock value, these scenes indicate that the implacable desire to speak, on the part of a black child, is dangerous and must be silenced. The opening scene of *Black Boy*, when the four-year-old Richard partially burns down the house, is rooted in the mother's warnings to Richard "to keep still," to "make no noise" (3). His childish delight in a bird "wheel[ing] past the window" yields an instinctive "glad shout" from the young boy, followed by a sharp reprimand from his mother (3). Bored and resentful of such censorship, Richard sets the curtains on fire, causing a conflagration. The results of his action silence him: "I was terrified; I wanted to scream but was afraid" (5). His revenge against his mother is effective, but he is momentarily silenced by the awareness that, without comprehending what exactly went wrong, he has committed a grievous error. Albert E. Stone reads this scene as a metaphorical first encounter with racism. Richard, who has fallen seriously ill after the fire and the beating he received for setting it, must "be kept quiet. . . . [his] very life depended on it" (*BB* 7), according to the family doctor. Stone notes that "[m]edical and social prescriptions are the same: a black child in Mississippi must be taught to keep quiet, not to pry or protest."[8] Stone states that Richard's "glad shout" "is virtually the last sound of joy to issue from the boy's lips in the whole story,"[9] indicating that from this point forward Richard's speech ceases to be an unmediated expression of his relation to the world's but now an interaction with a system fraught with misinterpretation, danger, and pain. Richard's desire to speak is shown to be bad, dangerous in its consequences, and ultimately life threatening for the speaker.

The episode in which Richard hangs the stray kitten illustrates how Richard's relationship to language will develop, emphasizes the dangers of self-expression, and shows a primitive strategy for overturning the silencing of the black self. Here we see a Richard who will be dangerously "bad" in his use and manipulation of language. After the family moves to Memphis, Wright writes of his father, "he became important and forbidding to me only when I learned that I could not make noise when he was asleep in the daytime. He was the lawgiver in our family and I never laughed in his presence" (*BB* 11). Richard's father silences him, much as his mother did in the episode which opens the book. When a stray kitten "set[s] up a loud, persistent meowing," the father bellows, "Kill that damn thing . . . Do anything, but get it away from here!" (*BB* 12). Richard, angered and resentful at his father's silencing, resolves to take his father literally and hangs the kitten. The deliberate and spiteful nature of Richard's use of language is emphasized by dialogues with his brother, mother, and father, each of whom accuses Wright of manipulating language. "He didn't mean for you to kill 'im," says his brother (*BB* 12). "You shut your mouth!" says his mother in response to Richard's claim that his father told him to do it (*BB* 13). "You know better than that!" says his father (*BB* 13). Richard considers himself to have triumphed: "I had made him believe that I had taken his words literally. He could not punish me now without risking his authority" (*BB* 13). Richard, however, knows exactly what he has done and that his reverse signifying is both powerful and dangerous.

The kitten in this episode stands symbolically for the deprived young Richard, in that it acts out all Richard's desires and takes the consequences. Richard is silenced and paid little attention in the house of his father. The kitten, with its animal lack of self-control, expresses Richard's desire to speak by meowing in the face of threats and echoes Richard's persistent hunger. "We fed it scraps of food and gave it water, but it still meowed" (*BB* 11). The kitten also expresses Richard's desire for attention: it "lingered, brushing itself against our legs, and meowing plaintively" (12). Thus when Richard decides to lynch the kitten, he symbolically acknowledges the danger of his desire for self-expression and expresses his anger at his silencing. He enacts the probable fate of a black person who speaks immoderately or incorrectly. The depiction of this incident in a completely African-American context—Richard has yet to encounter white racism—simultaneously expresses anger at the complicity of blacks in silencing themselves and indicts, through the metaphorical lynching, the real obscenity, white oppression.

In these opening episodes, Richard Wright establishes his youthful self as a devilish child, capable of doing enormous harm to himself and others through language. He also establishes, through the lynching scene, the obscenity of the current situation. Both episodes are linked to attempts to silence him, and both portray the disastrous consequences of disobedience; the desire to speak can literally kill a black child in the South. The use of language is bad, and, as Valerie Smith notes, "the autobiography is replete with episodes that remind Richard that his misappropriation of language has dramatic consequences."[10] Timothy Dow Adams has also noted Wright's consistent misspeaking and misconstruction in encounters with blacks and whites,[11] and Herbert Leibowitz emphasizes Richard's inability to control this language when he writes that "[w]ords would suddenly rise from dark corners of his [Wright's] mind and shock and offend his family."[12]

Wright links his first experiences of self-expression to literal profanity. In both the saloon and schoolyard scenes, Richard's positive experience of self-expression is based on foul language, a point crucial in Wright's negotiation with language as an African-American artist. In the saloon, young Richard is allowed to make as much noise as he wants without being punished: "I was put on the floor and I ran giggling and shouting among the yelling crowd" (BB 24). This scene could be read as a return to the glad shout of the opening scene, except that the environment is corrupted by alcohol and bad language. Richard, however, cannot tell the difference and only feels delighted that adults are listening to him:

A man called me to him and whispered some words into my ear and told me that he would give me a nickel if I went to a woman and repeated them to her. I told him that I would say them; he gave me the nickel and I ran to the woman and shouted the words. A gale of laughter went up in the saloon. . . .

From then on, for a penny or a nickel, I would repeat to anyone whatever was whispered to me. In my foggy, tipsy state the reaction of the men and women to my mysterious words enthralled me. I ran from person to person, laughing, hiccoughing, spewing out filth that made them bend double with glee. (*BB* 24)

Of this period, Wright recalls, "I saw more than I could understand and heard more than I could remember" (*BB* 25). Richard does not understand what he says or why it generates such a reaction, but he remembers the impact. He is "enthralled," addicted to "the reaction of the men and women to my mysterious words" as much as to the alcohol he is fed. Wright narrates this scene with a sadness born of hindsight, noting both the irresponsible behavior of the saloon patrons and the despair of his mother. "She beat me," he says of his mother, "then she prayed and wept over me, imploring me to be good, . . . all of which had no weight to my wayward mind" (*BB* 25). Despite the mature Wright's apparent sadness about this event, however, we cannot escape the fact that young Richard is delighted with his experience in the saloon. He experiences positive effects through bad language, and Wright's presentation of the event renders his younger self immune from the criticism or judgment of the reader by both suppressing the obscenity in the text and assuring us that he is ignorant of the actual meaning of the words.

Similarly, the effects of Richard's "soap words" are perfectly logical to the reader but create the critical distance necessary for Wright to claim "bad" language as positive self-expression. First, Richard's experience in the saloon left him fascinated with words, and he "would thumb through the pages" of his playmates' schoolbooks "and question them about the baffling black print" (*BB* 25). Wright has realized the power of words, although he cannot discriminate between good and bad language. Thus his first day at school is a revelation, since he learns the meanings of the words he had repeated in the saloon. Though "frightened speechless" (*BB* 28) by actual schoolwork, during recess Richard has the pleasant surprise of learning he is quite precocious in some areas of knowledge:

> During that noon hour I learned all the four-letter words describing physiological and sex functions, and discovered that I had known them before—although I had not known what they meant. A tall black boy recited a long, funny piece of doggerel, replete with filth, describing the physiological relations between men and women, and I memorized it word for word after having heard it once. (*BB* 28–29)

Wright takes pains during this episode to distinguish the language of the text and the language being discussed. The content of the schoolyard chatter is rendered in scholarly, multisyllabic word choices. Wright uses the term "physiological" twice, refers to sex and excretion as "functions," and identifies a dirty rhyme by its literary name, "doggerel." Narrative distance notwithstanding, however, young Richard is delighted to know more about the words which had fascinated the saloon patrons, and he "memorized it [the dirty poem] word for word after having heard it once." Wright's younger self claims bad language as a source of positive self-expression, acceptable to his schoolyard peers as well as drinking adults.

He does not hesitate to put his new knowledge to use: "I gobbled my cold food that had been left covered on the table, seized a piece of soap and rushed into the streets, eager to display all I had learned in school since morning. I went from window to window and printed in huge soap-letters all my newly acquired four-letter words" (*BB* 29). Wright calls his work "inspirational scribblings" disparagingly, but young Richard was clearly *inspired* by this language and expected nothing but pleasure in deploying it. When his mother forces him to scrub off every word, to the tittering speculation of the neighborhood, Wright says, "I scrubbed at the four-letter soap-words and grew blind with anger" (*BB* 29). This scene is the literary equivalent of washing his mouth out with soap, "the first occasion on which the words he writes are publicly censored, the first incident during which family members and neighbors become angry, if amused, because of the words he writes."[13] Wright's anger results not from his mother's disbelief that he had learned the terms at school, but from the censorship of self-expression and the designation of his language as "bad." "Never again did I write words like that," notes Wright. "I kept them to myself" (*BB* 30). While readers can comprehend the motivation of the community in this scene, we can also see, from Richard's perspective, how the ideas of bad language and self-expression are connected to and prohibited by the black community.

But these experiences of self-expression through bad language not only teach Richard that he can speak but that his speech is not appropriate. The African-American community teaches him the joy of self-expression, but it also reminds him forcibly that self-expression is "bad" and censors it. For Wright to develop as an artist, he must learn to be "bad" with "good" language. Wright accomplishes this feat by first linking "bad" language to Richard's experiences with literature as a province controlled by whites; and then by showing that literature can be manipulated for the purposes of African-American self-expression. An examination of the scene where his grandmother whips him for telling her to "kiss back there," sandwiched between Richard's early encounters with imaginative literature, reveals the connection between these two forces. Richard and his brother are playing as they bathe, to the annoyance of Granny:

"Come here, you Richard!" Granny said, putting her knitting aside.

I went to her, walking sheepishly and nakedly across the floor. She snatched the towel from my hand and began to scrub my ears, my face, my neck.

"Bend over," she ordered.

I stooped and she scrubbed my anus. My mind was in a sort of daze, midway between daydreaming and thinking.

Then, before I know it, words—words whose meaning I did not fully know—had slipped out of my mouth.

"When you get through, kiss back there," I said, the words rolling softly but unpremeditatively.

My first indication that something was wrong was that Granny became terribly still, then she pushed me violently from her. I turned around and saw that her white face was frozen, that her black, deep-set eyes were blazing at me unblinkingly. Taking my cue from her queer expression, I knew that I had said something awful, but I had no notion just how awful it was. (BB 47–48)

Wright still represses what he actually said—"back there" is clearly a euphemism—thus indicating that he has not gained full control over bad language. Instead, he eroticizes the scene, working against the euphemism to titillate the reader. In short, Wright's imaginative reconstruction of this scene intimates Granny's nightmare of "foul practices." Richard approaches his Granny "sheepishly and nakedly." She orders him to bend over, and we are told, in graphic medical terms, that she began to scrub his anus. "Softly," the words "roll" off his tongue in a semiconscious state, the elements of play and violence blending to create an erotic echo in the text.

This scene gains force because Granny associates Richard's language with his taste in imaginative literature. Granny calls Richard's desire to read and to write "Devil stuff" (BB 45) and "the Devil's work" (BB 198). The washing scene occurs directly after Granny prevents Ella, a schoolteacher boarding with the family, from telling the story of "Bluebeard and His Seven Wives" to an enraptured Richard. "You stop that, you evil gal. . . . I want none of that Devil stuff in my house!" (BB 45), Granny screams, equating imaginative literature with evil, but Richard is already fascinated. "You're going to burn in hell," his grandmother tells him when he insists on hearing the end of the story. Following the washing scene, Ella moves out, "weeping and distraught," since "Granny said emphatically that she knew who had ruined me, that she knew I had learned about 'foul practices' from reading Ella's books, and when I asked what 'foul practices' were, my mother beat me afresh" (*BB* 52). In Richard's young mind, the love of imaginative literature and the use of bad language are intimately connected. Despite Wright's obvious disdain for his grandmother's opinion, he does not psychologically escape from the association of self-expression and literature with bad language.

Wright associates the creation and enjoyment of literature with white oppression. Young Richard, who needs money to buy food, takes on a paper route that seems to satisfy his desire to read as well. His friend, "a tall, black rebellious boy who was bright in his studies and yet utterly fearless in his assertion of himself" (*BB* 149), seems to have much in common with Richard, since the boy's father will not let him read fiction. The two boys cement their friendship over the most enticing aspect of selling these papers, a magazine supplement included with the paper featuring stories such as "Riders of the Purple Sage." Unfortunately, the paper is a propaganda vehicle for the Ku Klux Klan, and the material surrounding the innocuous story clearly demonstrates the political power of language. Although Wright, the narrator, warns from the beginning that "the newspaper was thin, ill-edited and designed to circulate among rural, white Protestant readers" (*BB* 150), it is not until a "tall, quiet, soft-spoken black man" explains, very gently, the content of the paper that Richard realizes that his love of literature is a guilty pleasure. As Granny forewarned, imaginative literature becomes "the Devil's work." This episode also establishes that literature and language, as controlled by whites, can co-opt the unwitting; Richard should beware of the context of literature, beware that the literature he enjoys is not necessarily meant to help him. The danger of perceived co-option is clear: alienation from the black community. As the man tells Richard, "A lot of folks wanted to speak to you about these papers, but they were scared. They thought you were mixed up with some white Ku Kluxers and if they told you to stop you would put the Kluxers on 'em" (*BB* 155).

Richard's first published work, "The Voodoo of Hell's Half-

Acre," cements his alienation from the black community. This situation is most clearly stated with his school fellows:

> My schoolmates could not understand why anyone would want to write a story; and, above all, they could not understand why I had called it *The Voodoo of Hell's Half-Acre*. The mood out of which a story was written was the most alien thing conceivable to them. They looked at me with new eyes, and a distance, a suspiciousness came between us. If I had thought anything in writing the story, I had thought that perhaps it would make me more acceptable to them, and now it was cutting me off from them more completely than ever. (*BB* 197)

As Horace Porter succinctly put it, "The problem is the young artist's radical disassociation of sensibility from that of the group."[14] His schoolmates come to him with the same "baffled eyes" (*BB* 196) his neighbor turned to him when Richard read her his sketch of the Indian girl: "When I finished she smiled at me oddly, her eyes baffled and astonished" (*BB* 141). The "distance" and "suspiciousness" develops from written proof of Richard's desire for self-expression through language. The word "hell" in the title excites comment because it doubly marks Richard as an inappropriate user of language and a user of inappropriate language. Within the family, his story is considered blasphemy; Granny reduces his creative work to "a lie" and "the Devil's work" (*BB* 198), and Aunt Addie and Uncle Tom want to know why he would use the word "hell" in the title. Even his mother thinks he might appear "weak-minded" for writing stories, an ironic reversal of the strong-mindedness his use of language reveals.

Richard exceeds the boundaries placed on language use by African Americans when he writes his story because he believes that language can be used properly by blacks to express their individuality. Richard sought admiration for his exceptional skill in producing a story, perhaps seeking a response similar to that of his neighbor to his sketch of the Indian girl: "Her inability to grasp what I had done or was trying to do somehow gratified me" (*BB*

142). He also hoped to show his family that language was capable of good, justifying his fiction as he did his hymn verses: "I justified this by telling myself that, if I wrote a really good hymn, Granny might forgive me. But I failed even in that; the Holy Ghost was simply nowhere near me" (*BB* 140). But Wright is unable to account for his determination to write out his individuality, asking, "where had I got this notion of doing something in the future, of going away, from home and accomplishing something that would be recognized by others?" (*BB* 199). His explanation glosses Frederick Douglass's claim that education, or self-expression, is precisely what is kept from African Americans to keep them in their place: "I was building up in me a dream which the entire educational system of the South had been rigged to stifle. I was feeling the very thing that the state of Mississippi had spent millions of dollars to make sure that I would never feel."[15] His desire to write, to express himself, is obscene, a taboo for blacks "upon which the penalty of death had been placed." He marks himself as part of a black literary tradition of protest through literature, and he makes himself a marked man in both the white and black communities. When he hears his Uncle Tom speaking to his cousin Maggie and saying, "Didn't I tell you to stay away from him? That boy's a dangerous fool, I tell you!" (*BB* 204), a "flash of insight" (BB 205) reveals to him his relation to his family and to his community. Griggs emphasizes his alienation when he tells Richard that "White people make it their business to watch niggers. . . . And they pass the word around. . . . You're marked already" (*BB* 217). Indeed, Richard is known for saying "just one short sentence too many" (*BB* 231).

Once Richard arrives in Memphis, he begins to analyze the language barriers put in place by racism. He knows that when a white man however well-intentioned he may be, says to him, "Say, boy, I'm from the North," his remark must be interpreted against the dangerous background of race language: "With one sentence he had lifted out of the silent dark the race question and I stood on the edge of a precipice" (*BB* 272–73). He knows that the North is part of the catalog of "topics that southern white men did not like to discuss with Negroes" (*BB* 272). Wright is highly aware of the hazards of misinterpreting white language and the massive impact it can have on relations between blacks, as the fight with Harrison shows. Although each boy assures the other that the white men are trying to make them fight by spreading false rumors, they are unable to resist fully the linguistic mastery of the whites who weave a story around them.

Faced with this web of language, Richard Wright mangages to subvert white language by literally reading his way into the white culture, and then twisting it. He makes their language "bad" by redirecting it as he did his father's admonition to kill the kitten. Acquiring a reading list from H. L. Mencken's *A Book of Prefaces*, Wright finds in these texts strategies that refigure his relationship to language and to whites. When Wright says of Sinclair Lewis's *Main Street*, "[i]t made me see my boss, Mr. Gerald, and identify him as an American type. . . . I had always felt a vast distance separating me from the boss, and now I felt closer to him, though still distant" (*BB* 294), he not only approaches equality through literature but turns the idea of labeling through language around to negate the individuality of Mr. Gerald, who becomes a "Babbitt." Wright also begins to find expression for his mother's pain in Dreiser's *Jennie Gerhart* and *Sister Carrie*. He twists the white authors' words to find an understanding and expression of his own culture, taking the traditions of realism and naturalism for himself. This transformation is nothing less than theft, a theft and redirection of language punishable by death.[16] As one of Wright's white co-workers remarks, "You act like you've stolen something" (*BB* 296). The white man's use of a theme commonly used to denigrate the black community—that they are naturally predisposed to steal—is laughably transparent in this context, since what Wright has stolen is the ability to use language powerfully, the ability to make his bad language heard through the manipulation of white text. Like Frederick Douglass, Richard Wright has fully exposed the racist structure around him: "I no longer *felt* that the world about me was hostile, killing; I *knew* it" (*BB* 296).

Wright's model for transforming and redirecting definitions of bad and good language comes from the writing of H. L. Mencken, whose project in *A Book of Prefaces* is similar to Wright's in *Black*

Boy. Wright decides that Mencken must be doing something right with the language if the white southern newspapers have heaped their "hardest words"—"fool"—on him (*BB* 288). On opening the book, Wright says,

> I was jarred and shocked by the style, the clear, clean, sweeping sentences. Why did he write like that? And how did one write like that? I pictured the man as a raging demon, slashing with his pen, consumed with hate, denouncing everything American, extolling everything European or German, laughing at the weaknesses of people, mocking God, authority. What was this? I stood up, trying to realize what reality lay behind the meaning of the words. . . . Yes, this man was fighting, fighting with words. He was using words as a weapon, using them as one would use a club. Could words be weapons? Well, yes, for they were here. Then, maybe, perhaps, I could use them as a weapon? No. It frightened me. I read on and what amazed me was not what he said, but how on earth anybody had the courage to say it. (*BB* 293)

Mencken is "baaad." He has made words into weapons, words that strike and curse, just as Wright will try to do with his work. Throughout *Black Boy*, Wright's depiction of himself encourages us to see in him a "raging demon." His grandmother berated and beat him for his deviltry and blasphemy. *Black Boy* also contains its share of "laughing at the weaknesses of people, mocking God, [and] authority." Richard has at times seemed "consumed with hate," lashing out with curses against the oppression that holds him hostage. Mencken provides Wright with his first intimation that it might be possible to "hurl words into his darkness and wait for an echo, and if an echo sounded, no matter how faintly, I would send other words to tell, to march, to fight" (*BB* 453).

At the end of *Black Boy*, Richard Wright absconds with the goods, as it were escaping north to begin his writing career in earnest. Yet the timeline of *Black Boy*, and its continuation in *American Hunger*, does not bring Wright's life up to the time of publication for the autobiography. The chronicle ends prior to the publication of Wright's novels, while he is still a member of the

Communist party. Thus the autobiographical text ends before Richard Wright the author has been recognized as such; the author of *Native Son* has yet to publish a book. His articulate self—the author Baldwin imagines "shouting curses"—is still in hiding.

Critics have suggested that *Black Boy* may be an authenticating text for *Native Son*, explaining how Wright created Bigger Thomas, the protagonist of *Native Son*, and how he escaped "*becoming* a Bigger."[17] *Black Boy* is also seen as a complement to *How "Bigger" Was Born*, an authenticating text that prefaced some editions of *Native Son*. While "*Bigger*" provides the sociological authentication for the novel, *Black Boy* authenticates the "extraordinary articulate self" behind *Native Son*, according to Robert Stepto.[18] But the "self" and the "author" do not coincide in *Black Boy*, raising the possibility that Wright was not ready to take on his authorial self as an autobiographical self in 1945. To expose himself as an author would too closely connect him to his stated goals in writing *Native Son*.

Native Son aroused ire among whites and blacks, and the fact that Wright had to justify his protagonist with a separate text indicates considerable discomfort in the public's reaction to the text.[19] The African-American author ran the risk of ostracism by both African-American and white communities if he were found guilty of portraying the black experience inappropriately.

In *How "Bigger" Was Born*, Wright admits his concern that the subject matter of *Native Son* might be considered bad, both by whites and blacks. "Like Bigger himself," Wright wrote:

> I felt a mental censor—product of the fears a Negro feels from living in America—standing over me, draped in white, warning me not to write. This censor's warnings were translated into my own thought processes thus, "What will white people think if I draw the picture of such a Negro boy? Will they not at once say: 'See, didn't we tell you all along that niggers are like that? Now, look, one of their own kind has come along and drawn the picture for us!' "[20]

Wright's inner censor is "draped in white," thus raising the possibility that the actual censor is black, an African-American com-

munity which has specific "race uplift" goals. While Wright op-
poses the "I" and the white censor, the censor comes clearly from
within the race, from an African-American community aware of
how easily African-American expression can be co-opted by whites
to fit damaging sterotypes.

Wright also admits in this text that he has both manipulated
the "good" language of whites and begun to utter curses at white
oppression in *Native Son*. As he describes in *Black Boy*, Wright manipulated white experience and imagination to create Bigger.

> Let me give examples of how I began to develop the dim
> negative of Bigger. I met white writers who talked of their
> responses, who told me how whites reacted to this lurid Amer-
> ican scene. And, as they talked, I'd translate what they said in
> terms of Bigger's life. But what was more important still, I read
> their novels. Here, for the first time, I found ways and tech-
> niques of gauging meaningfully the effects of American civili-
> zation upon the personalities of people. I took these tech-
> niques, these ways of seeing and feeling, and twisted them,
> bent them, adapted them, until they became *my* ways of ap-
> prehending the locked-in life of the Black Belt areas.[21]

Bigger is partially white, invested with white literary strategies
that are "twisted" and "bent" until they reflect the oppressed
consciousness. Wright makes "good" literature "bad" in the
African-American sense. While this passage can support a claim
for the universality of Bigger's experience, it presents stronger
evidence that Wright stole the literature and privileged white experience and turned it into a curse, *Native Son*. Wright specifically
states in "*Bigger*" that he began *Native Son* as a sort of curse against
the white authorities running the South Side Boys' Club, "an
institution which tried to reclaim the thousands of Bigger Thomases from the dives and alleys of the Black Belt."[22] Feeling like he
was doing "dressed up police work" by working at the club,
Wright looked forward to the evening, when he thought, "Go to
it, boys! Prove to the bastards that gave you these games that life
is stronger than ping-pong."[23] *Native Son* thus becomes a rebellious

text, working against the assimilation of the Bigger Thomases of the world.

But autobiography, a self-conscious expression of the self, presents greater personal risks than fiction for the African-American author because it involves the self in the political system of language. Wright's first attempt at autobiography, an informal talk given at Fisk University, left him not only conscious of the possible power of his autobiography, but also terrified:

> After the speech I stood sweating, wanting to get away. A Negro educator came rushing down the aisle, his face tight with emotion. "Goddam," he panted in a whisper, "you're the first man to tell the truth in this town."[24]

While the Negro educator reacted positively to Wright's personal statement, the prose reminds us of the visceral terror Wright feels before the judgment of African-American and white listeners. Wright is "sweating," and the Negro educator is "rushing down the aisle, his face tight with emotion." Until the educator opens his mouth, there is the possibility that Wright's words were received like his decision to write his own speech for high school graduation. The expression of the black self directly, nonfictionally, through language is still terrifying to Wright despite his literary success.

Given his admissions about the goals of *Native Son*, perhaps Wright could not afford to expose his fully developed authorial self in autobiography. He could not assume the language strategies of the "author" in the pose of "autobiographer." By holding the authorial self in abeyance, Wright measures a distance that prevents a judgment on whether his language, and therefore his self, is "good" or "bad."

Notes

1. James Baldwin, "Everybody's Protest Novel," in *Notes of a Native Son* (New York: Dial, 1963), 21–22.

2. Richard Wright, *Black Boy* (New York: Harper Perennial, 1993), hereafter cited parenthetically in the text as *BB*. To avoid confusion, I refer to the protagonist of *Black Boy* as "Richard" and the writer as "Wright." Wright-as-narrator articulates some of Richard's experiences with greater consciousness of racial issues than Richard would have been capable of at the time.

3. In *Cursing in America* (Philadelphia: Benjamins, 1992), Timothy Jay divides the notion of "bad" language into ten categories: cursing, profanity, blasphemy, taboo, obscenity, vulgarity, slang, epithets, insults and slurs, and scatology. Most of these catagories make their appearance during the course of *Black Boy*. In his analysis, Jay uses the terms "cursing" and "dirty words" interchangeably to refer to inappropriate or offensive language. I follow his method, using the terms *bad language, cursing,* and *dirty words* to designate inappropriate language in the text.

4. Frederick Douglass, "Narrative of the Life of Frederick Douglass, an American Slave," in *The Classic Slave Narratives,* ed. Henry Louis Gates, Jr. (New York: New American Library, 1987), 274.

5. Tony Thorne, "bad," in *The Dictionary of Contemporary Slang* (New York: Pantheon, 1990), 20.

6. Zora Neale Hurston, *Dust Tracks on a Road* (New York: Harper Perennial 1991), 127–28.

7. Horace Porter, "The Horror and the Glory: Wright's Portrait of the Artist in *Black Boy* and *American Hunger*," in *Richard Wright: Critical Perspectives Past and Present,* ed. Henry Louis Gates, Jr., and K. A. Appiah (New York: Amistad, 1993), 316.

8. Albert E. Stone, "The Childhood of the Artist: Louis Sullivan and Richard Wright," in *Autobiographical Occasions and Original Acts* (Philadelphia: University of Pennsylvania Press, 1982), 128.

9. Ibid., 125.

10. Valerie Smith, "Alienation and Creativity in the Fiction of Richard Wright," in Gates and Appiah, *Richard Wright,* 437.

11. Timothy Dow Adams, " 'I Do Believe Him though I Know He Lies': Lying as Genre and Metaphor in *Black Boy*," in Gates and Appiah, *Richard Wright,* 312–13.

12. Herbert Leibowitz, " 'Arise, Ye Pris'ners of Starvation': Richard Wright's *Black Boy* and *American Hunger*," in Gates and Appiah, *Richard Wright,* 331.

13. Porter, "Horror and the Glory," 321.

14. Ibid., 323.

15. Douglass, "Narrative," 199.

16. Wright's strategy here foreshadows his 1957 essay "The Literature of the Negro in the United States," in *White Man, Listen!* (New York: Doubleday, 1964), in which he "steals" Pushkin and Dumas from the white canon by exposing their racial heritage. He argues that in the United States, where anyone with any black ancestry is considered "black," these authors would be considerd black. In revealing the instability of racial categorization and literary canonization. Wright undercuts notions both of what Negro literature is and what the (white) Western canon is.

17. Robert Stepto, *From Behind the Veil: A Study of Afro-American Narrative* (Urbana: University of Illinois Press, 1979).

18. Ibid.

19. *Black Boy* was also subject to such accusations. In a review of the novel, Sinclair Lewis argued that "placidly busy white reviewers" and "a couple of agitated Negro reviewers" castigated Wright for "too much 'emotion,' too much 'bitterness.' " In Gates and Appiah, *Richard Wright*, 30–31.

20. Richard Wright, *How "Bigger" Was Born* (New York, 1940), xxxiii.

21. Ibid., xxvi.

22. Ibid., xl.

23. Ibid., xli.

24. Stone, "Childhood," 120.

Richard Wright

"Wearing the Mask"

TIMOTHY ADAMS

❖ ❖ ❖

An autobiography is the truest of all books; for
while it inevitably consists mainly of extinctions
of the truth, shirkings of the truth, partial revelations of the truth, with hardly an instance of
plain straight truth, the remorseless truth is there,
between the lines.

—Mark Twain

L IKE THE AUTOBIOGRAPHIES of Gertrude Stein and
Sherwood Anderson, Richard Wright's *Black Boy*, published in
1945, has confused readers because of its generic ambiguity. For
many readers, the book is particularly honest, sincere, open, convincing, and accurate. But for others, *Black Boy* leaves a feeling of
inauthenticity, a sense that the story or its author is not to be
trusted. These conflicting reactions are best illustrated by the following representative observations by Ralph K. White and W. E. B.
Du Bois. White, a psychologist, has identified "ruthless honesty"
as "the outstanding quality which made the book not only moving but also intellectually satisfying."[1] But Du Bois notes that
although "nothing that Richard Wright says is in itself unbelievable or impossible; it is the total picture that is not convincing."[2]
Attempting to reconcile these opposing views, I wish to argue
that both sides are correct: that the book is an especially truthful
account of the black experience in America, even though the
protagonist's story often does not ring true, and that this inability

to tell the truth is Wright's major metaphor of self. A repeated pattern of misrepresentation becomes the author's way of making us believe that his personality, his family, his race—his whole childhood and youth—conspired to prevent him from hearing the truth, speaking the truth, or even being believed unless he lied.

For most readers, worries about *Black Boy*'s trustworthiness stem from questions of genre. Although the book was clearly not called "The Autobiography of Richard Wright," its subtitle—"A Record of Childhood and Youth"—does suggest autobiography with some claim to documentary accuracy. The following descriptions of *Black Boy* reflect the confusion of readers: biography, autobiographical story, fictionalized biography, masterpiece of romanced facts, sort of autobiography, pseudoautobiography, part-fiction/part-truth autobiography, autobiography with the quality of fiction, and case history.[3]

Some of these generic confusions were generated by Wright's statements about his intent. Although he meant the work to be a collective autobiography, a personalized record of countless black Americans growing up with a personal history of hunger, deprivation, and constant racism, he seems to have realized as he wrote that his own life was not a very characteristic one and that he was focusing as much on his particular problems as on a typical black childhood. Wright decided to write his life story after giving an autobiographical talk to a racially mixed audience at Fisk University in Nashville, Tennessee, in 1943. After the talk, Wright noted that he "had accidentally blundered into the secret black, hidden core of race relations in the United States. That core is this: nobody is ever expected to speak honestly about the problem. . . . And I learned that when the truth was plowed up in their faces, they shook and trembled and didn't know what to do."[4] A year later, Wright used the same metaphor when he wrote, "The hardest truth to me to plow up was in my own life."[5] But speaking honestly about a racism endemic throughout America was more complicated, for author and for reader, than Wright could have known, and a more delicate instrument than a plow would be needed for harvesting the past. Using truthfulness as his watchword, Wright began *Black Boy* as an attempt to correct the record of black history, including his personal one, which already consisted of a number of "biographies of the author" or "notes on contributors" that were written by himself in the third person, sometimes with exaggerated accounts of his youth. In several interviews, as well as in his "The Ethics of Living Jim Crow," an autobiographical sketch originally published in 1937 in *American Stuff: WPA Writers' Anthology*, Wright had already given an incorrect birth date and had begun to establish a history over-emphasizing the negative aspects of his early life.[6]

Most revelatory about the conflict between his intentions and the actual writing of his personal narrative is the following observation by Wright from a newspaper article called "The Birth of *Black Boy*":

> The real hard terror of writing like this came when I found that writing of one's life was vastly different from speaking of it. I was rendering a close and emotionally connected account of my experience and the ease I had had in speaking from notes at Fisk would not come again. I found that to tell the truth is the hardest thing on earth, harder than fighting in a war, harder than taking part in a revolution. If you try, you will find that at times sweat will break upon you. You will find that even if you succeed in discounting the attitudes of others to you and your life, you must wrestle with yourself most of all, fight with yourself; for there will surge up in you a strong desire to alter facts, to dress up your feelings. You'll find that there are many things that you don't want to admit about yourself and others. As your record shapes itself an awed wonder haunts you. And yet there is no more exciting an adventure than trying to be honest in this way. The clean, strong feeling that sweeps you when you've done it makes you know that.[7]

Although Wright seemed unsure of his book's generic identity, he never referred to *Black Boy* as autobiography. His original title, *American Hunger*, later used for the portion of his life story that began after leaving Memphis for Chicago, came after he had rejected *The Empty Box, Days of Famine, The Empty Houses, The Assassin, Bread and Water,* and *Black Confession,* all of which sound like titles for novels.[8] When his literary agent suggested the subtitle "The Biography of a Courageous Negro," Wright responded with "The Biography of an American Negro," then with eight other possibilities including "Coming of Age in the Black South," "A Record in Anguish," "A Study in Anguish," and "A Chronicle of Anxiety." Such titles indicate his feeling that the book he had written was less personal, more documentary—a study, a record, a chronicle, or even a biography—than autobiography.[9] Constance Webb reports that Wright was uneasy with the word autobiography, both because of "an inner distaste for revealing in first person instead of through a fictitious character the dread and fear and anguishing self-questioning of his life" and because he realized that he would write his story using "portions of his own childhood stories told him by friends things he had observed happening to others," and fictional techniques.[10]

Although some readers believe Wright gave in to the "strong desire to alter facts" and "to dress up" his feelings, the book's tendency to intermix fiction and facts is clearly part of both Wright's personal literary history and the Afro-American literary tradition in which he was writing. The form of *Black Boy* in part imitates the traditional slave narrative, a literary type that allowed for a high degree of fictionality in the cause of abolition.[11] A number of major works of literature by black Americans, such as Du Bois's *The Souls of Black Folks,* Toomer's *Cane,* and Johnson's *The Autobiography of an Ex-Coloured Man,* feature mixtures of genres; and Wright, simultaneously a poet, novelist, essayist, journalist, playwright, and actor, often used the same material in different genres. For example, "The Ethics of Living Jim Crow" first appeared as an essay and was later attached to the stories of *Uncle Tom's Children,* one of which, "Bright and Morning Star," is retold in *Black Boy* as a tale that held the protagonist in thrall, even though he "did not know if the story was factually true or not."[12] When "black boy" says that the story is emotionally true, he reflects exactly the kind of truth Wright wants his readers to respond to in *Black Boy*. Some of the characters in *Black Boy* have been given fictional names, whereas Bigger Thomas, the central character in the fictional *Native Son*, is the real name of one of Wright's acquaintances.[13] That he used real names in fiction and fictional names in nonfiction is typical of Richard Wright, who further confounded the usual distinctions between author and persona by playing the role of Bigger Thomas in the first film version of *Native Son*.

Richard Wright makes clear that *Black Boy* is not meant as a traditional autobiography by presenting much of the story in the form of dialogue marked with quotation marks, a technique that suggests the unusual degree of fiction within the story. Although critics often point to Wright's first novel, *Native Son* (1940), as the other half of *Black Boy*, another model for this autobiographical work was his more recently completed *Twelve Million Black Voices: A Folk History of the American Negro in the United States* (1941). Writing *Black Boy* in the spirit of folk history seemed a reasonable thing to do, and Wright apparently saw no hypocrisy in omitting personal details that did not contribute to what he was simultaneously thinking of as his own story and the story of millions of others. Wright's claim to be composing the autobiography of a generic black child is reinforced by the narrator's particular reaction to racism: "The things that influenced my conduct as a Negro did not have to happen to me directly; I needed but to hear of them to feel their full effects in the deepest layers of my consciousness" (190).

Roy Pascal may be right in asserting that "where a lie is the result of a calculated intention to appear right or important, danger is done to autobiographical truth" and that "the most frequent cause of failure in autobiography is an untruthfulness which arises from the desire to appear admirable."[14] However, most of the omission in *Black Boy* is designed not to make the persona appear admirable but to make Richard Wright into "black boy," to underplay his own family's middle-class ways and more positive values. Wright does not mention that his mother was a successful schoolteacher and that many of his friends were children of college faculty members; he omits most of his father's family background and his own sexual experiences. Also mainly left out are reactions from sensitive southern whites, including those of the Wall family to whom, we learn from Michel Fabre's biography, "he sometimes submitted his problems and plans . . . and soon considered their house a second home where he met with more understanding than from his own family."[15]

In addition to omissions, name changes, poetic interludes, and extensive dialogue, *Black Boy* is replete with questionable events that biographical research has revealed to be exaggerated, inaccurate, mistaken, or invented. The section of Fabre's biography dealing with the *Black Boy* years is characterized by constant disclaimers about the factuality of the story. Some omissions can be explained because the urbane ex-Communist who began *Black Boy* "wanted to see himself as a child of the proletariat," though "in reality he attached greater importance to the honorable position of his grandparents in their town than he did to his peasant background."[16] Although these distortions are acceptable to many, especially in light of Wright's intention of using his life to show the effects of racism, numerous other manipulations are less acceptable because they are more self-serving.

Most of these incidents are relatively minor and might be judged unimportant; however, the misrepresentations in two of the book's most important episodes—the high school graduation speech and the story of Uncle Hoskins and the Mississippi River—might be less acceptable. "Black boy's" refusal to deliver the principal's graduation speech rather than his own is apparently based on truth, but the version in *Black Boy* leaves out the important fact that Wright rewrote his speech, cutting out more volatile passages, as a compromise.[17] The story of Uncle Hoskins does not ring true, for how could a boy whose life had been so violent to that point be scared of his uncle's relatively harmless trick? He says of his Uncle Hoskins, "I never trusted him after that. Whenever I saw his face the memory of my terror upon the river would come back, vivid and strong, and it stood as a barrier between us" (47). One reason the tale feels false is that the whole story—complete with the above revelations about Uncle Hoskins—actually happened to Ralph Ellison, who told it to Richard Wright.[18]

For many critics, including Edward Margolies, these deliberate manipulations reduce *Black Boy*'s authenticity as autobiography because they set up doubts about everything, the same doubts that resonate through the remarks of black writers from Du Bois to Baldwin to David Bradley, all of whom have persisted in taking *Black Boy*'s protagonist to be Richard Wright.[19] But "Richard Wright is not the same person as the hero of that book, not the same as 'I' or 'Richard' or the 'Black boy,' not by several light years," argues James Olney, who refers to the book's chief character as "black boy," explaining that "by means of an encompassing and creative memory, Richard Wright imagines it all, and he is as much the creator of the figure that he calls 'Richard' as he is of the figure that, in *Native Son*, he calls 'Bigger . . .' "[20] Olney's idea that the central figure be treated as a single person referred to as "black boy," a literary character representing the actual author both as a child and as an adult—the famous writer imagining himself as representative of inarticulate black children—is finally convincing. That seems to be what Richard Wright meant to do, what he said he had done, and what he did.

Unlike that of Janet Cooke, who was labeled a liar for inventing a black boy in a series of articles in the *Washington Post* on drug use, . . . Richard Wright's approach is different: first, because he announces his intentions—in authorial statements external to the text and by title, quotation marks, use of symbolic and imagistic description, and well-organized plot—and second, because he is manipulating his own story, not someone else's. Ralph Ellison's review essay on *Black Boy*, "Richard Wright's Blues," begins with the refrain "If anybody ask you / 'who sing this song.' / Say it was ole [Black Boy] / done been here and gone,"[21] a blues singer's signature formula that clarifies two important facts about the book. First, the protagonist is a literary character named "black boy" who bears the same similarity to Richard Wright as the character Leadbelly, for example, does to the blues singer Huddie Ledbetter who sings about Leadbelly so often. Second, Ellison's refrain forewarns that the identity of the protagonist will be called into question by critics who will wonder who the elusive hero is and where he is going. Ellison sees *Black Boy* as a talking blues, but it is also a bebop jazz performance in which Wright uses his life as the melody on which to improvise.

Many critical objections to *Black Boy*'s methods of getting at the truth come from those who instinctively feel something strange about the work, not so much in its generic confusions as in its tone and in what Albert E. Stone, Jr., senses when he writes that "a proud and secret self presides over the text, covertly revealing itself through event, style, and metaphor."[22] When confronted with *Black Boy*'s deviations from absolute biographical truth, less-sophisticated readers, such as students, are seldom bothered. They sense that discrepancies uncovered by reading other texts have little bearing on the truth of the text at hand. Nevertheless, the same students often respond unfavorably to what they perceive as inauthenticity arising from within *Black Boy*. And part of their dislike of and distrust for "black boy" grows from the sense of our times that "narrative past . . . has lost its authenticating power," as Lionel Trilling observes. "Far from being an authenticating agent, indeed, it has become the very type of inauthenticity."[23] Caring little about the crossing of generic boundaries, students are disturbed by the idea that "life is susceptible of comprehension and thus of management," as Trilling further remarks.[24] In short, they are uncomfortable with *Black Boy*, not because it is not true, but because for them it does not ring true. They experience what Barrett John Mandel calls "dis-ease with the autobiography. It seems as if the author is lying (not, please, writing fiction), although readers cannot always easily put their finger on the lie."[25]

The lying that they sense centers on these three concerns: "black boy" is never wrong, falsely naive, and melodramatic, three characteristics of what Mandel refers to as autobiography in which "the ratification is negative—the light of now shines on the illusion the ego puts forth and reveals it as false."[26] Mandel believes that most autobiographers are basically honest, but those who are not give themselves away through tone: "Since the ego is in conflict with the truth, the reader very often gets that message. The author has created an illusion of an illusion. . . . The tone is forever slipping away from the content, giving itself away."[27] Although Mandel does not include *Black Boy* in the category of dishonest autobiographies, instead citing it as a typical reworking of the past, many critics have echoed the students' concerns. For example, Robert Stepto finds fault with two early incidents in which "black boy" insists on the literal meaning of words: when the character pretends to believe his father's injunction to kill a noisy kitten and when he refuses ninety-seven cents for his dog because he wants a dollar. "The fact remains that *Black Boy* requires its readers to admire Wright's persona's remarkable and unassailable innocence in certain major episodes, and to condone his exploitation of that innocence in others," writes Stepto. "This, I think, is a poorly tailored seam, if not precisely a flaw, in *Black Boy*'s narrative strategy."[28] Rather than seeing these episodes, and others like them, as examples of bad faith or as rough edges in the narrative fabric, I see them as deliberate renderings of the terrible dilemma of black boys and of their need to dissemble about everything, especially about the nature of their naiveté. Wright's persona is confessing, not boasting. His family life and his difficulty with hypocrisy made lying at once a constant requirement for survival and a nearly impossible performance, especially for a poor liar whose tone gives him away.

The inability to lie properly, exhibited in countless scenes, is "black boy's" major problem in adjusting to black-white relationships in his youth. Asked by a potential white employer if he steals, "black boy" is incredulous: "Lady, if I was a thief, I'd never tell anybody" (160), he replies. *Black Boy* is filled with episodes in which its hero is unable to lie, forced to lie, caught between conflicting lies, not believed unless he lies. Poorly constructed lies are appropriate metaphors to portray a boy whose efforts to set the record straight are as frustrated as his grandfather's futile attempts to claim a navy pension. Falsehoods are an apt metaphor for the speech of a boy who distrusts everyone, including himself.

Black Boy's opening, in which Wright describes how his four-year-old self set his grandmother's house on fire out of boredom and experimentation, is cited by virtually every commentator as an allegory for the fear, rebellion, anxiety, and need for freedom of the hero, as well as for the motifs of fire, hunger, and underground retreat. After the fire, which destroys more than half of the house, the child delivers this recollection:

> I was lashed so hard and long that I lost consciousness. I was beaten out of my senses and later I found myself in bed, screaming, determined to run away. . . . I was lost in a fog of fear. A doctor was called—I was afterwards told—and he ordered that I be kept abed, that I be kept quiet, that my very life depended upon it. . . . Whenever I tried to sleep I would see huge wobbly white bags, like the full udders of cows, suspended from the ceiling above me. Later, as I grew worse, I could see the bags in the daytime with my eyes open and I was gripped by the fear that they were going to fall and drench me with some horrible liquid. . . . Time finally bore me away from the dangerous bags and I got well. But for a long time I was chastened whenever I remembered that my mother had come close to killing me. (13)

Albert Stone perceptively notes that the last line of this passage represents "a striking reversal." "Where the reader expects a confession that the boy has tried (although inadvertently or unconsciously) to attack his own family, one finds the opposite. Such heavy rationalization clearly demands examination."[29] The adult autobiographer is not justifying setting houses on fire, rather, he is trying to show graphically and suddenly how distrustful a child of four had already become. The episode does not ring true because it is not necessarily literally true. In fact, Wright uses a contradictory description in "The Ethics of Living Jim Crow," written eight years earlier. Describing, in that essay, a cinder fight between white and black children, Wright claims he was cut by a broken milk bottle, rushed to the hospital by a kind neighbor, and later beaten by his mother until he "had a fever of one hundred and two. . . . All that night I was delirious and could not sleep. Each time I closed my eyes I saw monstrous white faces suspended from the ceiling, leering at me."[30] The cinder fight is retold in a later section of *Black Boy*, though in this version the hero's mother takes him to the doctor and beats him less severely.

The old-time musician Lily May Ledford in Ellesa Clay High's *Past Titan Rock: Journeys into an Appalachian Valley*, says, "I never tell a story the same way twice, but I tell the truth."[31] Similarly, Richard Wright has borrowed the rhetoric of the oral historian in consciously fictionalizing the story of the burning house and his subsequent punishment, at the same time sending signals that he has done so. Wright wants the reader to feel that something is not quite right about the whole scene. That the three-year-old brother can see the folly of playing with fire when the four-year-old "black boy" cannot, that the reasons for setting the fire are as spurious as the explanation ("I had just wanted to see how the curtains would look when they burned" [11]), that the nightmarish description of white bags filled with foul liquid is obviously meant to be symbolic, and finally that the boy is chastened, not by his actions, but by the thought that his mother had come close to killing him—all of these signals are meant to paint a truthful picture of a boy who later came to hold "a conviction that the meaning of living came only when one was struggling to wring a meaning out of meaningless suffering" (112).

The opening scene suggests the whole atmosphere of the book—a desperate fear of meaningless visitations of violence without context, a life of deliberate misrepresentations of the truth and complete distrust of all people, a world in which "each event spoke with a cryptic tongue" (14). Throughout *Black Boy*, Wright presents a lonely figure whose life does not ring true because "that's the way things were between whites and blacks in the South; many of the most important things were never openly said; they were understated and left to seep through to one" (188). Thus all actions are tempered by a subtext, which is obvious to everyone, a strategy that the author claimed to have discovered when he delivered his Fisk University oration.

Whenever the narrator questions his mother about racial relationships, she is defensive and evasive. "I knew that there was something my mother was holding back," he notes. "She was not concealing facts, but feelings, attitudes, convictions which she did not want me to know" (58), a misrepresentation that disturbs "black boy" who later says, "My personality was lopsided; my

knowledge of feeling was far greater than my knowledge of fact"
(136). Although the narrator holds back or conceals facts, he is
usually straightforward about emotional feelings, even though he
can say, "The safety of my life in the South depended upon how
well I concealed from all whites what I felt" (255). Worrying less
about factual truth, Wright was determined to stress the emotional truth of southern life to counteract the stereotypical myths
shown in the song that prefaced *Uncle Tom's Children*: "Is it true
what they say about Dixie? Does the sun really shine all the
time?"[32]

One of the ironies of *Black Boy* is that the narrator's constant
lying is emblematic of the truth that all black boys were required
not only to lie but to lie about their lying. In the boxing match
between "black boy" and a co-worker, this pattern is played out
almost mathematically. The two black boys are coerced into a
fight they both know is false, based on lies that are obvious to
all. Much of the shamefulness of the whole situation is that they
are forced to pretend that they are neither aware that the situation is false nor mindful that the whites know they know. These
paradoxes are clearly analyzed in Roger Rosenblatt's "Black Autobiography: Life as the Death Weapon": "They had been goaded
into a false and illogical act that somehow became logical and
true. At the end of their fight, Wright and Harrison *did* hold a
grudge against each other, just as their white supervisors had
initially contended." As a result, "a lie became the truth and . . .
two people who had thought they had known what the truth
was wound up living the lie."[33]

Although personal and institutional racism was everywhere
evident, southern whites generally maintained that they treated
blacks more humanely than did northern whites, that they understood blacks and knew how to deal with them, and that they
were friendly with blacks (as evidenced by their calling them by
their first names)—all of which blacks were supposed to pretend
they believed. Whites deliberately set up situations where blacks
were forced to steal; not only did they like to be stolen from, but
whites also forced blacks to lie repeatedly asking them if they
were thieves. "Whites placed a premium upon black deceit; they

encouraged irresponsibility; and their rewards were bestowed upon us blacks in the degree that we could make them feel safe and superior" (219), notes the narrator. When he forgets to call a white co-worker named Pease "Mister," he is caught in a trap from which the usual escape is "a nervous cryptic smile" (208). The boy's attempt to lie his way out of the situation fails, despite his ingenuity in turning the false accusation into an ambiguous apology:

> If I had said: No, sir, Mr. Pease, I never called you *Pease*, I would by inference have been calling Reynolds a liar; and if I had said: Yes, sir, Mr. Pease, I called you *Pease*, I would have been pleading guilty to the worst insult that a Negro can offer to a southern white man. I stood trying to think of a neutral course that would resolve this quickly risen nightmare. . . .
> "I don't remembering [*sic*] calling you *Pease*, Mr. Pease," I said cautiously, "and if I did, I sure didn't mean . . ."
> "You black sonofabitch! You called me *Pease*, then!" he spat, rising and slapping me till I bent sideways over a bench. (209)

Episodes like this make clear that an inability to tell the truth does not make black children into liars. Instead, the frequent descriptions of the protagonist as a prevaricator reveal to white readers the way blacks use lies to express truths, use, for example, the word *nigger* to mean one thing to white listeners, another to black. The elaborate system of signifying—of using words in exactly the opposite way from white usage (bad for good, cool for hot), of wearing the mask to cover emotions, of the lies behind the black children's game of dozens—is behind the motif of lying in *Black Boy*. Wright's metaphoric use of lying is made more complex by his awareness that a history of misrepresentation of true feelings made it difficult for black people to be certain when they were merely dissembling for protection, when they were lying to each other, or to themselves.

"There are some elusive, profound, recondite things that men find hard to say to other men," muses "black boy," "but with the Negro it is the little things of life that become hard to say, for these tiny items shape his destiny" (254). What sets the narrator apart from his black contemporaries is his difficulty with the lying that they find so easy: "In my dealing with whites I was conscious of the entirety of my relations with them, and they were conscious only of what was happening at a given moment. I had to keep remembering what others took for granted; I had to think out what others felt" (215).

The actual audience must narrow the gap between the narrative and authorial audiences; the reader of *Black Boy* must strive to be like the narrator of *Black Boy*, must keep what is happening at a particular moment and the entire history of black-white relations—the content and the context—together in his mind. Wright's context includes the need to speak simultaneously as an adult and as a child and to remove everything from his story that, even if it happened to be true, would allow white readers to maintain their distorted stereotype of southern blacks. He was searching for a way to confess his personal history of lying, forced on him by his childhood, while still demonstrating that he could be trusted by both black and white. His solution is what Maya Angelou calls "African-bush secretiveness":

> "If you ask a Negro where he's been, he'll tell you where he's going." To understand this important information, it is necessary to know who uses this tactic and on whom it works. If an unaware person is told a part of the truth (it is imperative that the answer embody truth), he is satisfied that his query has been answered. If an aware person (one who himself uses the stratagem) is given an answer which is truthful but bears only slightly if at all on the question, he knows that the information he seeks is of a private nature and will not be handed to him willingly.[34]

What makes *Black Boy* compelling is its ability to remain autobiography despite its obvious subordination of historicity. Although a reader may not be aware of the complexities of "black boy's" "African-bush" slanting of the truth or know about the book's fictionalizing, something, nevertheless, is unmistakably autobiographical about *Black Boy* that convinces even the unaware. What makes this true is the way the author signifies his lying through rhetoric, appeals in writing to both black and white, as he was unable to do in his speech in Nashville. One of the most significant patterns of the lying in the book involves just such a distinction between speaking and writing.

Wright's claim to be speaking for the millions of inarticulate children of the South is ironically reinforced by the constant difficulty the narrator has with the spoken, as opposed to the printed, word. Although a love of reading actually saves "black boy," he is constantly threatened by speaking. Often out of synchronization, he speaks when he should be quiet or is unable to utter a word when questioned; his words slip unaware from his mouth, flow out against his will. Just as often, he is verbally paralyzed, unable to produce a phrase. Early in life, he questions himself—"What on earth was the matter with me. . . . Every word and gesture I made seemed to provoke hostility" (158). He answers, toward the end of the book, "I knew what was wrong with me, but I could not correct it. The words and actions of white people were baffling signs to me" (215).

The problem with the spoken word begins with the narrator killing a kitten because of the pretense of not reading his father's command as figurative and continues with the melodramatic description of himself begging drinks as a six-year-old child, memorizing obscenities taught to him in a bar. Later "black boy" learns "all the four-letter words describing physiological and sex functions" (32) and yet claims to be astonished, while being bathed by his grandmother, at her reaction to his command: " 'When you get through, kiss back there,' I said, the words rolling softly but unpremeditatedly" (49). Wishing to recall those words, though only vaguely understanding why he is once again being punished so severely, "black boy" says, "None of the obscene words I had learned at school in Memphis had dealt with perversions of any sort, although I might have learned the words while loitering drunkenly in saloons" (53). This explanation is weak and unconvincing, especially given his earlier description of himself and other children stationing themselves for hours at the bottom of a series of outdoor toilets, observing the anatomies of their neighbors.

Forced to declare his belief in God by his family of Seventh Day Adventists, "black boy" misspeaks again and again. " 'I don't want to hurt God's feelings either,' I said, the words slipping irreverently from my lips before I was aware of their full meaning" (126). Trying to keep his grandmother from questioning him about religion, he hits upon the strategy of likening himself to Jacob, arguing that he would believe in God if he ever saw an angel. Although this plan is imagined with the purpose of "salving . . . Granny's frustrated feelings toward [him]" (128), the result is that his words are misconstrued. His grandmother thinks he has seen an angel, and "black boy" once again has "unwittingly committed an obscene act" (131). His explanation is another example of his difficulty with speaking as others did: "I must have spoken more loudly and harshly than was called for" (131).

Asked by a teacher to explain a schoolyard fight with two bullies, the protagonist says, "You're lying!" which causes the teacher to reply, even though "black boy" is right, "Don't you use that language in here" (137). Once again daydreaming, "black boy" interrupts his family "arguing some obscure point of religious doctrine" with a remark that he says "must have sounded reekingly blasphemous" (147). This time his grandmother is in bed for six weeks, her back wrenched in attempting to slap her grandson for his statements. Again "black boy" is an innocent victim, beaten for not allowing his grandmother to slap him— his physical, like his verbal skills, out of rhythm with his family. He is slapped for asking his grandmother, on a later occasion, what his dying grandfather's last words were and for replying to the question "What time have you?" with "If it's a little fast or slow, it's not far wrong" (173). "Black boy's" poor sense of timing makes him feel unreal, as if he "had been slapped out of the human race" (210), and causes him to resemble Ellison's "invisible man" who believes that such a condition "gives one a slightly different sense of time, you're never quite on the beat. Sometimes you're ahead and sometimes behind. Instead of the swift and imperceptible flowing of time, you are aware of its nodes, those points where time stands still or from which it leaps ahead."[35] Suggestive of the sense of time essential to jazz, these words describe the narrator who is out of phase with everyone until he can control the timing of his life through the syncopated rhythms of *Black Boy.*

In light of this repeated pattern—swift physical reprisal delivered to the totally astonished narrator for speaking out of turn—the following justification for threatening his aunt with a knife is surprising: "I had often been painfully beaten, but almost always I had felt that the beatings were somehow right and sensible, that I was in the wrong" (118). This confession sounds false because "black boy" never seems to admit that he is blameworthy for anything. "Nowhere in the book are Wright's actions and thoughts reprehensible," objects Edward Margolies, echoing a number of others.[36] Robert Felgar makes a similar point when he remarks that "the reader does tire of his persistent self-pity and self-aggrandizement."[37] An early reviewer argues that "the simple law of averages would prevent any one boy from getting into as many situations as we have related in this story, and one senses with regret, that it is hard to know where biography leaves off and fiction begins."[38] What these critics see as foolish self-pity is most apparent in the heavily melodramatic description of the familiar playground game of crack-the-whip, which the narrator describes in life-or-death terms: "They played a wildcat game called popping-the-whip, a seemingly innocent diversion whose excitement came only in spurts, but spurts that could hurl one to the edge of death itself. . . . The whip grew taut as human flesh and bone could bear and I felt that my arm was being torn from its socket" (122). Here the author is depicting a children's game using the kind of rhetoric usually reserved for a slave narrative— a cruel overseer whipping a runaway slave "to the edge of death."

Wright's words are not self-pitying; instead, he is presenting a naive youth who was never good at lying or exaggerating. The misrepresentation is so obvious that only a particularly inept liar would attempt it, a child who did not want to be good at lying. Only an outsider, such as "black boy," to the established systems of lying by both races, a representative of the many black adolescents then coming of age—what Wright hoped would be a new generation of the children of Uncle Tom, no longer willing to accept the old lie that the best way to fight racism was to lie through both omission and commission—could fail to distinguish between melodrama and genuine oppression and could be so surprised at the power of his words.

Black Boy should not be read as historical truth, which strives to report those incontrovertible facts that can be somehow corroborated, but as narrative truth. The story that Richard Wright creates in *Black Boy*, whatever its value as an exact historical record, is important both in telling us how the author remembers life in the pre-Depression South and in showing us what kind of person the author was in order to have written his story as he did. Although he is often deliberately false to historical truth, he seldom deviates from narrative truth. In *Black Boy*, Wright has made both the horrifyingly dramatic and the ordinary events of his life fit into a pattern, shaped by a consistent, metaphoric use of lying. "Interpretations are persuasive," argues Donald Spence, "not because of their evidential value but because of their rhetorical appeal; conviction emerges because the fit is good, not because we have necessarily made contact with the past."[39]

In *Black Boy*, Wright creates a version of himself whose metaphor for survival and for sustenance is falsehood. But the multiple lies of the narrator, like the fibs of children trying to avoid what they see as irrational punishment, are palpably obvious. These lies are not meant to deceive; they are deliberately embarrassing in their transparency. For the protagonist, whose home life was so warped that only when he lied could he be believed, Alfred Kazin's dictum—"One writes to make a home for oneself, on paper"[40]—is particularly true. The author's manipulations of genre and his metaphoric lies have produced a book about which Du Bois's assessment is, in my judgment, exactly backward: although much of what Richard Wright wrote is not literally true, the total picture is ultimately convincing, taken in context. For all of his lying, "black boy's" essential drive is for truth.

Notes

1. Ralph K. White, *"Black Boy*: A Value Analysis," *Journal of Abnormal and Social Psychology* 42 (1947): 442–43.

2. W. E. B. Du Bois, "Richard Wright Looks Back," in *Richard Wright: The Critical Reception*, ed. John M. Reilly (New York: Burt Franklin, 1978), 133.

3. For these terms, see the following in John M. Reilly, ed., *Richard Wright: The Critical Reception* (New York: Burt Franklin, 1978), 122–76: Gottlieb, Creighton, Du Bois, Garlington, Bentley, Richter, and Hamilton.

4. Quoted in Michael Fabre, *The Unfinished Quest of Richard Wright*, trans. Isabel Barzun (New York: Norton, 1973), 578.

5. Ibid.

6. Ibid., 250.

7. Quoted in Michel Fabre, afterword to *American Hunger*, by Richard Wright (New York: Harper and Row, 1977), 138.

8. Alternate titles cited in Constance Webb, *Richard Wright: A Biography* (New York: Putnam's 1968), 706–7, and in Charles T. Davis and Michel Fabre, *Richard Wright: A Primary Bibliography* (Boston: Hall, 1982), 56.

9. Fabre, *Unfinished Quest*, 259, 578.

10. Webb, *Richard Wright*, 198, 207–8.

11. For a discussion of *Black Boy* and slave narratives, see Robert B. Stepto, *From Behind the Veil: A Study of Afro-American Narrative* (Urbana: University of Illinois Press, 1979); Sidonie Smith, *Where I'm Bound: Patterns of Slavery and Freedom in Black Autobiography* (Westport, Conn.: Greenwood, 1974); and Steven Butterfield, *Black Autobiography in America* (Amherst: University of Massachusetts Press, 1974).

12. Richard Wright, *Black Boy: A Record of Childhood and Youth* (New York: Harper and Row, 1940), 83; subsequent citations appear within the text.

13. See Webb, *Richard Wright*, 402, and Richard Wright, "How 'Bigger' Was Born," in *Native Son* (New York: Harper and Row, 1940).

14. Roy Pascal, *Design and Truth in Autobiography* (Cambridge, Mass.: Harvard University Press, 1960), 63, 82.

15. Fabre, *Unfinished Quest*, 47.

16. Ibid., 6.

17. Ibid., 56.

18. Cited in Webb, *Richard Wright*, 419.

19. Edward Margolies, *The Art of Richard Wright* (Carbondale: Southern Illinois University Press, 1969), 16.

20. James Olney, "Some Versions of Memory / Some Versions of Bios: The Ontology of Autobiography," in *Autobiography: Essays Theoretical and Critical*, ed. James Olney (Princeton, N.J.: Princeton University Press, 1980), 244–45.

21. Ralph Ellison, "Richard Wright's Blues," in *Shadow and Act* (New York: American Library, 1966), 89.

22. Albert E. Stone, *Autobiographical Occasions and Original Acts: Versions of American Identity from Henry Adams to Nate Shaw* (Philadelphia: University of Pennsylvania Press, 1982), 124.

23. Lionel Trilling, *Sincerity and Authenticity* (Cambridge, Mass.: Harvard University Press, 1972), 139.

24. Ibid., 135.

25. Barrett John Mandel, "Full of Life Now," in *Autobiography: Essays Theoretical and Critical*, ed. James Olney (Princeton, N.J.: Princeton University Press, 1980), 65.

26. Ibid.

27. Ibid., 66.

28. Stepto, *From Behind the Veil*, 143.

29. Stone, *Autobiographical Occasions*, 126.

30. Richard Wright, "The Ethics of Living Jim Crow," in *Uncle Tom's Children* (New York: Harper, 1940), 4–5.

31. Ellesa Clay High, *Past Titan Rock: Journeys into an Appalachian Valley* (Lexington: University Press of Kentucky, 1984), 65.

32. Richard Wright, *Uncle Tom's Children* (New York: Harper, 1940), 2.

33. Roger Rosenblatt, "Black Autobiography: Life as the Death Weapon," in *Autobiography*, ed. Olney, 173.

34. Maya Angelou, *I Know Why the Caged Bird Sings* (New York: Bantam, 1971), 164.

35. Ralph Ellison, *Invisible Man* (New York: Random House, Vintage, 1972), 8.

36. Margolies, *Art of Richard Wright*, 16.

37. Robert Felgar, *Richard Wright* (Boston: Twayne, 1980), 46.

38. Patsy Graves, "Opportunity," in *Richard Wright: The Critical Reception*, ed. John M. Reilly (New York: Burt Franklin, 1978), 173.

39. Donald Spence, *Narrative Truth and Historical Truth* (New York: Norton, 1982), 31.

40. Alfred Kazin, "The Self as History: Reflections on Autobiography," in *Telling Lives: The Biographer's Art*, ed. Marc Pachter (Washington, D.C.: New Republic Books/National Portrait Gallery, 1979), 89.

The Horror and the Glory

Richard Wright's Portrait of the Artist in Black Boy and American Hunger

HORACE A. PORTER

◆　◆　◆

A S THE CURTAIN FALLS on the final page of *American Hunger*, the continuation of Richard Wright's autobiography, *Black Boy*, he is alone in his "narrow room, watching the sun sink slowly in the chilly May sky." Having just been attacked by former Communist associates as he attempted to march in the May Day parade, he ruminates about his life. He concludes that all he has, after living in both Mississippi and Chicago, are "words and a dim knowledge that my country has shown me no examples of how to live a human life." Wright ends his autobiography with the following words:

> I wanted to try to build a bridge of words between me and that world outside, that world which was so distant and elusive that it seemed unreal.
>
> I would hurl words into this darkness and wait for an echo, and if an echo sounded, no matter how faintly, I would send other words to tell, to march, to fight, to create a sense of the

hunger for life that gnaws in us all, to keep alive in our hearts a sense of the inexpressibly human.[1]

American Hunger (1977) is the continuation of *Black Boy* (1945). Wright initially composed them as one book entitled *The Horror and the Glory*. Thus, a reading of the two volumes as one continuous autobiography is crucial for a comprehensive understanding of his portrayal of himself as a young writer. Wright achieves remarkable poetic closure by bringing together at the end of *American Hunger* several interrelated themes which he elaborately spells out in *Black Boy*. The passage cited above illustrates his concern for words, his intense and troubling solitude, and his yearning to effect a revolution in the collective consciousness of America through the act of writing. In a sentence, the end of *American Hunger* is essentially the denouement of *Black Boy*.

Although critics have discussed the effect of Wright's early life on his writings, none has shown systematically how *Black Boy* (and to a lesser degree *American Hunger*) can be read primarily as a portrait of the artist as a young man. Consequently, I intend to demonstrate how the theme of words (with their transforming and redeeming power) is the nucleus around which ancillary themes swirl. Wright's incredible struggle to master words is inextricably bound to his defiant quest for individual existence and expression. To be sure, the fundamental nature of the experience is not peculiar to Wright. Many, if not most, writers are marked by their experience with words during childhood. It is no accident that, say, Jean-Paul Sartre, a writer whom Wright eventually meets and admires, entitles his autobiography *Les Mots*. What one sees in Wright's autobiographies is how the behavior of his fanatically religious grandmother, the painful legacy of his father, the chronic suffering of his mother, and his interactions with blacks and whites both in and outside his immediate community are all thematically connected to the way Wright uses words to succeed as a writer and as a man.

The first chapter of *Black Boy*, the first scene, foreshadows the major theme—the development of the young artist's sensibility—of the book. Wright begins his narrative by recounting how he

set fire to his house when he was four years old. His is a conflagration sparked by an odd combination of boredom, curiosity,
and imagination. One day Wright looks yearningly out into the
empty street and dreams of running, playing, and shouting. First,
he burns straws from a broom; then, his temporary pyromania
getting the better of him, he wonders how "the long fluffy white
curtains" would look if he lit them: "Red circles were eating into
the white cloth; then a flare of flames shot out. . . . The fire soared
to the ceiling. . . . Soon a sheet of yellow lit the room."[2] Then,
most terrifying of all, Wright runs outside and hides in "a dark
hollow of a brick chimney and balled [himself] into a tight knot."[3]
Wright's aim in hiding under the burning house was to avoid the
predictable whipping by his mother. Moreover, his four-year-old
imagination is so preoccupied with the effect of his derring-do
that he does not realize that his own life is on a burning line.
Hiding beneath the house and thinking of the possible consequences of his actions—the death of family members—Wright
states: "It seemed that I had been hiding for ages, and when the
stomping and screaming died down, I felt lonely, cast forever out
of life."[4]

Wright may not have been completely aware of the psychological import of his opening scene. For, it appears that we must
interpret young Wright's act of arson for what it really may have
been. Perhaps even at that early age he was trying to free himself
from the tyranny of his father's house in which his fanatically
religious grandmother ruled: "I saw the image of my grandmother
lying helplessly upon her bed and there were yellow flames in
her black hair."[5] The fact that young Wright has these thoughts
while in "a dark hollow of a brick chimney . . . balled . . . into a
tight knot," raises more profound psychological issues. Does this
image represent a yearning to return to the womb? Does it constitute symbolic parricide? Does it symbolize the possibility of a
new birth? When Wright sets his father's house aflame, he also
makes an eloquent statement against the world the southern
slaveholders had made. Wright's later anxiety and guilt over
having turned his back on his father's world drives him to write.
His autobiography is an act of self-assertion and self-vindication

in which he fearlessly confronts his father. Moreover, he demonstrates his love for his mother. And he pays homage to the anonymous, illiterate blacks whose world he fled.

In the process of moving away from his family and community, Wright began experiencing the problem (a consuming sense of loss and abandonment) that was to become central to his life and his work. In certain primary respects, he was surely cognizant of the problem, but it operated on levels sufficiently profound as to be unfathomable later in his career. Numerous passages in *Black Boy* illustrate the phenomenon.

What has been characterized as ritual parricide comes readily to mind when Wright's father is awakened one day by the meowing of a stray cat his sons have found. Wright's father screams at him and his brother: "Kill that damn thing!" His father shouts, "Do anything, but get it away from here!" Ignoring the advice of his brother, Wright does exactly what his father suggests. He puts a rope around the cat's neck and hangs it. Why? Wright explains:

> I had had my first triumph over my father. I had made him believe that I had taken his words literally. He could not punish me now without risking his authority. I was happy because I had at last found a way to throw criticism of him into his face. I had made him feel that, if he whipped me for killing the kitten, I would never give serious weight to his words again. I had made him know that I felt he was cruel and I had done it without his punishing me.[6]

Young Wright's cunning act of interpretation is the telling point here. If one were dubious about the meaning of the son's act of arson, the passage cited above demonstrates a full-blown hatred and contempt. But note how Wright focuses on his father's words, how he attempts to neutralize his father's psychological authority by a willful misinterpretation of his statement.

At the end of the first chapter of *Black Boy*, Wright banishes his father from the remaining pages of both volumes of his autobiography. His father eventually deserts his mother, and she struggles to support her two sons. On one occasion when Wright and his mother pay his father and his "strange woman" a visit in order to obtain money for food, Wright's father hands him a nickel. Wright refuses to accept the nickel, his father laughs and puts the nickel back in his pocket, stating, "That's all I got." That image of his father was indelibly etched in Wright's memory. Wright states that over the years, his father's face would "surge up in my imagination so vivid and strong that I felt I could reach out and touch it; I would stare at it, feeling that it possessed some vital meaning which always eluded me."[7]

Wright does not see his father for "a quarter of a century" after that encounter. His reunion with his father after a prolonged period leads to one of the more poignant and profound meditations of the autobiography. Staring at "the sharecropper, clad in ragged overalls, holding a muddy hoe in his gnarled, veined hands," Wright sees his biological father, but he also sees another man. The man standing before him is now both more and less than his father:

> My mind and consciousness had become so greatly and violently altered that when I tried to talk to him I realized that, though ties of blood made us kin, though I could see a shadow of my face in his face, though there was an echo of my voice in his voice, we were forever strangers, speaking a different language, living on vastly different planes of reality. . . . I stood before him, pained, my mind aching as it embraced the simple nakedness of his life, feeling how completely his soul was imprisoned by the slow flow of the seasons, by wind and rain and sun, how fastened were his memories to a crude and raw past, how chained were his actions and emotions to the direct, animalistic impulses of his withering body. . . . I forgave him and pitied him as my eyes looked past him to the unpainted wooden shack. From far beyond the horizon that bound this bleak plantation there had come to me through my living the knowledge that my father was a black peasant who had gone to the city seeking life, but who had failed in the city, and who at last fled the city—that same city which had lifted me

in its burning arms and borne me toward alien and undreamed
of shores of knowing.[8]

In the foregoing meditation, Wright depicts his father as a
"sharecropper," a "black peasant," whose actions and emotions
are "chained . . . to the direct, animalistic impulses of his . . .
body." He and his father are "forever strangers, speaking a different language." Even in this passage, which ostensibly has little to
do with language, Wright reminds us that his ability to use and
understand words has transformed him. His mind and consciousness have been "greatly and violently" altered. So Wright finally
achieves the kind of authority he longed for as a kid. His father
is no longer the threatening figure who told him to kill the
kitten. From Wright's point of view, he has become something
other; now, he is more phenomenon than person. Thus, Wright
is simultaneously compassionate and dispassionate. On the one
hand, he forgives his father; on the other, he clearly indicates
that certain bonds between him and his father have been irrep-
arably severed.

Wright's mother also plays an important role in this psychological scheme of reconciliation and vindication. Despite the fact
that his mother whipped him until he was unconscious after he
set the house afire, he expresses tenderness toward her throughout *Black Boy*; Wright informs the reader that his mother was the
first person who taught him to read and told him stories. After
Wright hanged the kitten in order to triumph over his father, he
explains that his mother, who is "more imaginative, retaliated
with an assault upon my sensibilities that crushed me with the
moral horror involved in taking a life."[9] His mother makes him
bury the kitten that night and makes him pray.

Wright's mother not only instructs him in the high moral
values of civilized society, but she also teaches him how to survive
in a hostile and impoverished environment. She teaches him "the
ethics of living Jim Crow." She frequently whips him because she
knows that certain small gestures of self-pride and assertion
would lead readily to brutality or death. Thus, if Wright's

mother's arm is sometimes the arm of the oppressive social order, that same arm is, ironically, the tender, loving arm of the parent, nurturing and protecting her young. She instructs him in those traditions of black life that are sustaining—the necessity of learning to persevere, the ability to maintain grace under pressure, the practice of containing one's pain. Small wonder that Wright sees in his mother's suffering and in her will to live in spite of her rapidly declining health a symbol of the numerous ills and injustices of the society in which they both live:

> My mother's suffering grew into a symbol in my mind, gathering to itself all the poverty, the ignorance, the helplessness; the painful, baffling, hunger-ridden days and hours; the restless moving, the futile seeking, the uncertainty, the fear, the dread; the meaningless pain and the endless suffering. Her life set the emotional tone of my life, colored the men and women I was to meet in the future, conditioned my relation to events that had not yet happened. . . . A somberness of spirit that I was never to lose settled over me during the slow years of my mother's unrelieved suffering, a somberness that was to make me stand apart and look upon excessive joy with suspicion, that was to make me self-conscious, that was to make me keep forever on the move, as though to escape a nameless fate seeking to overtake me.[10]

Wright, the loving son, feels powerless before the seemingly vast impersonal forces which break his mother's spirit and ruin her health. His mother's life becomes a psychological and emotional charge to him; the "vital meaning" inherent in her suffering is the unstated psychological instruction to dedicate his life to the amelioration of the ills and injustices of society in whatever manner he finds appropriate and effective. Had Wright become indifferent toward the symbol of suffering his mother's life represents, his indifference would have been in effect psychological and moral betrayal of the first order. However, his reflections on his mother's suffering profoundly change his whole attitude at

the tender age of twelve. The spirit he catches sharpens the edges
of his inchoate, artistic sensibility. We witness the writer's personality assuming self-conscious definition:

> The spirit I had caught gave me insight into the suffering of
> others, . . . made me sit for hours while others told me of their
> lives. . . . It made me love burrowing into psychology, into re-
> alistic and naturalistic fiction and art. . . . It directed my loyal-
> ties to the side of men in rebellion; it made me love talk that
> sought answers to questions that could help nobody, that
> could only keep alive in me that enthralling sense of wonder
> and awe in the face of the drama of human feeling which is
> hidden by the external drama of life.[11]

Furthermore, the symbol of Wright's mother's suffering gives
him hope. Long before he leaves the South he dreams of going
north in order to "do something to redeem my being alive":

> I dreamed of going North and writing books, novels. The
> North symbolized to me all that I had not felt and seen; it
> had no relation whatever to what actually existed. Yet, by
> imagining a place where everything was possible, I kept hope
> alive in me. But where had I got this notion of doing some-
> thing in the future, of going away from home and accomplish-
> ing something that would be recognized by others? I had, of
> course, read my Horatio Alger stories, and I knew my Get-
> Rich-Quick Wallingford series from cover to cover, though I
> had sense enough not to hope to get rich. . . . yet I felt I had
> to go somewhere and do something to redeem my being alive.[12]

Note that Wright considers the writing of books or novels as the
activity which would give his life meaning—"redeem my being
alive."

In the preceding pages, we discussed the subtle psychological
question of Wright's relationship to his parents. The task now is
to demonstrate specifically how Wright uses words to remove

himself from the oppressive community which tries to stifle his imagination. Over the years, Wright becomes increasingly defiant and articulate. And the members of his southern community become suspicious of his goals and motives. Words lead to Wright's salvation and to his redemption. From the first pages of *Black Boy*, the reader witnesses Wright at the tender, impressionable age of six becoming a messenger of the obscene. One day a black man drags Wright, who is peering curiously through the doors of a saloon, inside. The unscrupulous and ignorant adults give him liquor and send obscene messages by him back and forth to one another. Wright goes from one person to the next shouting various obscenities in tune to the savage glee and laughter of the crowd. Surely, the incident makes Wright, inquisitive as he is, wonder about the odd effects of his words.

He later learns his first lesson on the power of the written word. Returning home after his first day of school during which he had learned "all the four-letter words describing physiological and sex functions" from a group of older boys, he decides to display his newly acquired knowledge. Wright goes from window to window in his neighborhood and writes the words in huge soap letters. A woman stops him and drives him home. That night the same woman informs his mother of what Wright calls his "inspirational scribblings." As punishment, she takes him out into the night with a pail of water and a towel and demands that he erase the words he had written: " 'Now scrub until that word's gone,' she ordered."

This comical incident may appear insignificant on the surface. Furthermore, one cannot know the nature or the degree of the psychological effect the incident had on Wright. However, it seems reasonable to assume that it had a significant psychological impact. As Wright presents it, it is the first occasion on which words he writes are publicly censored, the first incident during which family members and neighbors become angry, if amused, because of words he writes. Wright states: "Neighbors gathered, giggling, muttering words of pity and astonishment, asking my mother how on earth I could have learned so much so quickly. I scrubbed at the four-letter soap words and grew blind with anger."[13]

Wright's first written words are not the only words to get him in trouble. His first exposure to imaginative literature also causes a scene. One day a young schoolteacher, who boards with his grandmother, reads to him "Bluebeard and His Seven Wives." Wright describes the effect that the story has on him in visionary terms: "The tale made the world around me be, throb, live. As she spoke reality changed, the look of things altered, and the world became peopled with magical presences. My sense of life deepened and the feel of things was different, somehow. Enchanted and enthralled."[14]

Wright's visionary, enchanted state does not last. His grandmother screams, "You stop that you evil gal! . . . I want none of that devil stuff in my house!" When Wright insists that he likes the story and wants to hear what happened, his grandmother tells him, "You're going to burn in hell." Wright reacts strongly to this incident. He promises himself that when he is old enough, he "would buy all the novels there were and read them." Not knowing the end of the tale fills Wright with "a sense of emptiness and loss." He states that the tale struck "a profoundly responsive chord" in him:

> So profoundly responsive a chord had the tale struck in me that the threats of my mother and grandmother had no effect whatsoever. They read my insistence as mere obstinacy, as foolishness, something that would quickly pass; and they had no notion how desperately serious the tale had made me. They could not have known that Ella's whispered story of deception and murder had been the first experience in my life that had elicited from me a total emotional response. No words or punishment could have possibly made me doubt. I had tasted what to me was life, and I would have more of it somehow, some way.[15]

This passage dramatizes one of the central conflicts of Wright's autobiography. It shows, on the one hand, Wright's literary pre-

cocity and illustrates, on the other, how his days with his grandmother led to one psychological scrimmage after another. The
grandmother loathes what she considers to be Wright's imperti-
nence. No matter, given Wright's thirst for knowledge, his longing to achieve a self-conscious, independent manhood, his intense
desire to live in a world elsewhere, he proves to be extremely
vigilant in his fight against those, including his grandmother, his
uncle, his aunt, and his high school principal, whom he calls his
"tribal" oppressors. To Wright, theirs is at worst the path to poverty and ignorance and at best a path to what Mann's Tonio
Kröger calls "the blisses of the commonplace." Wrights wants
neither.

Reflecting on his grandmother's insistence that he join the
church and walk in the path of righteousness (as she sees it),
Wright states: "We young men had been trapped by the community, the tribe in which we lived and which we were a part.
The tribe for its own safety was asking us to be at one with it."[16]
Moreover, commenting on how the community views anyone
who chooses not to have his soul saved, Wright asserts:

> This business of saving souls had no ethics; every human re-
> lationship was shamelessly exploited. In essence, the tribe was
> asking us whether we shared its feeling; if we refused to join
> the church, it was equivalent to saying no, to placing ourselves
> in the position of moral monsters.[17]

It is important to keep in mind that Wright's mother is an
exception. To be sure, she shares many of the views of the community, but out of love, she aids Wright in his attempt to escape
the tribe. Speaking of his mother after the Bluebeard incident,
Wright says: "I burned to learn to read novels and I tortured my
mother into telling me the meaning of every strange word I saw,
not because the word itself had any value, but because it was the
gateway to a forbidden and enchanting land."[18]

Against the wishes of the community, Wright continues to
read and develop as a young writer. His first real triumph comes
when the editor of the local Negro newspaper accepts one of

Wright's stories, "The Voodoo of Hell's Half-Acre." The plot of
the story involves a villain who wants a widow's home. After the
story is published, no one, except the newspaper editor, gives any
encouragement. His grandmother calls it "the devil's work"; his
high school principal objects to his use of "hell" in the story's
title; even his mother feels that his writing will make people feel
that he is "weak minded." His classmates do not believe that he
has written the story:

> They were convinced that I had not told them the truth. We
> had never had any instruction in literary matters at school;
> the literature of the nation of the Negro had never been men-
> tioned. My schoolmates could not understand why I had called
> it *The Voodoo of Hell's Half-Acre.* The mood out of which a story
> was written was the most alien thing conceivable to them.
> They looked at me with new eyes, and a distance, a suspicious-
> ness came between us. If I had thought anything in writing
> the story, I had thought that perhaps it would make me more
> acceptable to them, and now it was cutting me off from them
> more completely than ever.[19]

Herein, Wright identifies another problem which menaces him
throughout his writing life. The problem is the young artist's
radical disassociation of sensibility from that of the group. In this
regard, he is reminiscent of the young artist heroes of Mann and
Joyce, of Tonio Kröger and Stephen Dedalus. However, Wright's
plight as a young artist is significantly different in a crucial way.
His is not simply the inability to experience, by dint of his poetic
sensibility, "the blisses of the commonplace." Not only is Wright
pitted against his immediate family and community, the tribe, as
he calls them. He must also fight against the prejudices of the
larger society.

Wright wrote "The Voodoo of Hell's Half-Acre" when he was
fifteen. He concludes:

> Had I been conscious of the full extent to which I was pushing
> against the current of my environment, I would have been
> frightened altogether out of my attempts at writing....

I was building up in me a dream which the entire educational system of the South had been rigged to stifle. I was feeling the very thing that the state of Mississippi had spent millions of dollars to make sure that I would never feel; I was becoming aware of the thing that the Jim Crow laws had been drafted and passed to keep out of my consciousness; I was acting on impulses that Southern senators in the nation's capital had striven to keep out of Negro life.[20]

A telling example which brilliantly demonstrates what Wright means in the passage cited above involves his love for words and books once again. When Wright is nineteen, he reads an editorial in the Memphis *Commercial Appeal* which calls H. L. Mencken a fool. Wright knows that Mencken is the editor of the *American Mercury*, and he wonders what Mencken has done to deserve such scorn. How can he find out about Mencken? Since blacks are denied the right to use the public libraries, he is not permitted to check out books. But Wright proves both ingenious and cunning.

He looks around among his co-workers at the optical company where he is employed and chooses the white person—a Mr. Falk—who he thinks might be sympathetic. The man is an Irish Catholic, "a pope lover," as the white southerners say. Wright had gotten books from the library for him several times, and wisely figures that since he too is hated, he might be somewhat sympathetic. Wright's imagination and courage pay off. Although somewhat skeptical about Wright's curious request from the outset, Mr. Falk eventually gives Wright his card, warning him of the risk involved and swearing him to secrecy. Wright promises that he will write the kind of notes Mr. Falk usually writes and that he will sign Falk's name.

Since Wright does not know the title of any of Mencken's books, he carefully composes what he considers a foolproof note: "*Dear Madam: Will you please let this nigger have some books by H. L. Mencken.*"[21] The librarian returns with Mencken's *A Book of Prefaces* and *Prejudices*. His reading of Mencken provides him with a formidable reading list: Anatole France, Joseph Conrad, Sinclair Lewis, Sherwood Anderson, Dostoyevsky, George Moore, Flaubert,

Maupassant, Tolstoy, Frank Harris, Twain, Hardy, Crane, Zola, Norris, Gorky, Bergson, Ibsen, Shaw, Dumas, Poe, Mann, Dreiser, Eliot, Gide, Stendhal, and others. Wright starts reading many of the writers Mencken mentions. Moreover, the general effect of his reading was to make him more obsessive about it: "Reading grew into a passion. . . . Reading was like a drug, a dope."[22]

Mencken provides Wright with far more than a convenient reading list of some of the greater masters. He becomes an example to Wright—perhaps an idol—both in matters of style and vocational perspective or stance:

> I opened *A Book of Prefaces* and began to read. I was jarred and shocked by the style, the clear, clean, sweeping sentences. Why did he write like that? And how did one write like that? I pictured the man as a raging demon, slashing with his pen, consumed with hate, denouncing everything American, extolling everything European or German, laughing at the weaknesses of people, mocking God, authority. What was this? I stood up, trying to realize what reality lay behind the meaning of the words. . . . Yes, this man was fighting, fighting with words. He was using words as a weapon, using them as one would use a club. Could words be weapons? Well, yes, for here they were. Then, maybe, perhaps, I could use them as a weapon.[23]

A few months after reading Mencken, Wright finds the convenient opportunity to flee to the North. He closes *Black Boy* on an optimistic note.

American Hunger opens with Wright's arrival in Chicago and with the din of that windy city entering his consciousness, mocking his treasured fantasies. Wright had envisioned Chicago as a city of refuge. However, his first years are "long years of semi-starvation." He works as a dishwasher, part-time post office clerk, life insurance salesman, and laboratory custodian. Since none of these jobs lasts long, finding adequate food and shelter becomes extremely difficult. At one point, Wright shares a windowless rear room with his mother and younger brother. But good luck occasionally comes in the guise of ill. Many of the experiences he has while working odd jobs supplies revelations which subsequently form the core of his best fiction. Wright probably would not have written *Native Son* if he had not seen and felt Bigger Thomas's rage.

The first half of *American Hunger* is primarily devoted to a sociopsychological portrayal of Wright's life and work among the black and white poor. Wright shows how ignorance and racial discrimination fuel prejudice and self-hatred. He gives us glimpses of *les miserables*, who are corrupted, exploited, and destroyed. While working as an insurance salesman, Wright himself aids in the swindling of the black poor. Yet we are aware throughout that his is a form of predatory desperation. His is the hard choice between honesty and starvation.

Communists dominate the second half of *American Hunger*. As Wright tells his story, he has strong reservations about the party from the outset and gets involved indirectly. He becomes a member of the party primarily because he is a writer, and he leaves it for the same reason. Lacking intellectual communion and meaningful social contacts, he joins Chicago's John Reed Club. The members enthusiastically welcome him, and he is immediately given a writing assignment for *Left Front*. After only two months and due to internal rivalry, Wright is elected executive secretary of the club. He humbly declines the nomination at first but, after some insistent prodding, reluctantly accepts the position. Thus, though not a Communist, he heads one of the party's leading cultural organizations. Given his independence of mind, however, he raises too many troubling questions for party officials, and they soon begin to wage a war against him. They try to harness his imagination and whip it down the official ideological path. But Wright is already at work on the stories of his first book, *Uncle Tom's Children*. He writes: "Must I discard my plot ideas and seek new ones? No. I could not. My writing was my way of seeing, my way of living, my way of feeling, and who could change his sight, his notion of direction, his senses?"[24]

Wright dwells rather tediously on the Communist party in the six brief chapters of *American Hunger*. However, he does devote limited space to the story of how he "managed to keep humanly alive through transfusions from books" and the story of how he learned his craft: "working nights I spent my days in experimental writing, filling endless pages with stream-of-consciousness Negro dialect, trying to depict the dwellers of the Black Belt as I felt and saw them."[25] And ever conscious of the need to refine his craft, Wright moved into other realms. He read Stein's *Three Lives*, Crane's *The Red Badge of Courage*, and Dostoyevsky's *The Possessed*. He strove to achieve the "dazzling magic" of Proust's prose in *A Remembrance of Things Past*. "I spent hours and days pounding out disconnected sentences for the sheer love of words. . . . I strove to master words, to make them disappear, to make them important by making them new, to make them melt into a rising spiral of emotional stimuli, each feeding and reinforcing the other, and all ending in an emotional climax that would drench the reader with a sense of a new world. That was the single aim of my living."[26]

Finally Wright was able to redeem himself with words. They moved him from Mississippi to Chicago to New York and eventually made Paris his home town. Using words, he hurled himself at the boundary lines of his existence. Goethe's saying "man can find no better retreat from the world than art, and man can find no stronger link with the world than art" sums up the conundrum of Wright's life.

Notes

1. Richard Wright, *American Hunger* (New York: Harper and Row, 1977), 135. It is unfortunate that *American Hunger* is such a late arrival. Its chief value is that it brings together for the first time in book form the second half of Wright's original autobiography, most of which was published in essay form in the *Atlantic Monthly* (August and September 1944), in the anthology *Cross Section* (1945), and in the September 1945 issue of *Mademoiselle*. Therefore, *American Hunger* is hardly new and surely not a lost literary treasure fortuitously blown into public view by heaven's four winds. In any case, whatever the reason for its belated, posthumous publication, it has been effectively robbed of its capacity to affect significantly the public's mind. For despite the power of *Black Boy* and *Native*

Son, they are now part and parcel of a bygone era. For a thorough discussion of this matter, see Jerry W. Ward, "Richard Wright's Hunger," *Virginia Quarterly Review* (Winter 1978): 148–53.

2. Richard Wright, *Black Boy* (New York: Harper & Brothers, 1945), 4.
3. Ibid.
4. Ibid., 5.
5. Ibid.
6. Ibid., 10–11.
7. Ibid., 30.
8. Ibid., 30–31.
9. Ibid., 11.
10. Ibid., 87.
11. Ibid.
12. Ibid., 147.
13. Ibid., 22.
14. Ibid., 34.
15. Ibid., 36.
16. Ibid., 134.
17. Ibid.
18. Ibid., 135.
19. Ibid., 146.
20. Ibid., 148.
21. Ibid., 216.
22. Ibid., 218–19.
23. Ibid., 218.
24. Wright, *American Hunger*, 93.
25. Ibid., 24.
26. Ibid., 25.

Suggested Reading

Aaron, Daniel. *Writers on the Left*. New York: Avon, 1965.

Baker, Houston A., Jr. *Blues, Ideology, and Afro-American Literature*. Chicago, IL: University of Chicago Press, 1984.

Brignano, Russell C. *Richard Wright: An Introduction to the Man and His Works*. Pittsburgh: University of Pittsburgh Press, 1970.

Butler, Robert. *Native Son: The Emergence of a New Black Hero*. Boston: Twayne, 1991.

Fabre, Michel. *Richard Wright: Books and Writers*. Jackson: University Press of Mississippi, 1990.

———. *The Unfinished Quest of Richard Wright*. 2d ed. Urbana: University of Illinois Press, 1993.

———. *The World of Richard Wright*. Jackson: University Press of Mississippi, 1985.

Fabre, Michel, and Charles T. Davis. *Richard Wright: A Primary Bibliography*. Boston: Hall, 1982.

Gates, Henry Louis, Jr., and K. A. Appiah, eds. *Richard Wright: Critical Perspectives Past and Present*. New York: Amistad, 1993.

Gayle, Addison. *Richard Wright: Ordeal of a Native Son*. Garden City, NY: Doubleday, 1980.

Hakutani, Yoshinobu, ed. *Critical Essays on Richard Wright*. Boston: Hall, 1982.

——. *Richard Wright and Racial Discourse*. Columbia: University of Missouri Press, 1996.

Joyce, Joyce Ann. *Richard Wright's Art of Tragedy*. Iowa City: University of Iowa Press, 1986.

Kinnamon, Keneth. *The Emergence of Richard Wright: A Study in Literature and Society*. Urbana: University of Illinois Press, 1973.

Kinnamon, Keneth, and Michel Fabre, eds. *Conversations with Richard Wright*. Jackson: University Press of Mississippi, 1993.

Kinnamon, Keneth, with Joseph Benson, Michel Fabre, and Craig Werner. *A Richard Wright Bibliography: Fifty Years of Criticism and Commentary, 1933–1982*. Westport, CT: Greenwood, 1988.

McCall, Dan. *The Example of Richard Wright*. New York: Harcourt, Brace, & World, 1969.

Macksey, Richard, and Frank E. Moorer, eds. *Richard Wright: A Collection of Critical Essays*. Englewood Cliffs, NJ: Prentice Hall, 1984.

Margolies, Edward. *The Art of Richard Wright*. Carbondale: Southern Illinois University Press, 1969.

Miller, Eugene E. *Voice of a Native Son: The Poetics of Richard Wright*. Jackson: University Press of Mississippi, 1990.

Mitchell, Hayley, ed. *Readings on "Black Boy."* San Diego, CA: Greenhaven, 2000.

Naison, Mark. *Communists in Harlem during the Depression*. Urbana: University of Illinois Press, 1983.

Rampersad, Arnold, ed. *Richard Wright: A Collection of Critical Essays*. Englewood Cliffs, NJ: Prentice Hall, 1995.

Rowley, Hazel. *Richard Wright: The Life and Times*. New York: Holt, 2001.

Walker, Margaret. *Richard Wright: Daemonic Genius*. New York: Amistad, 1988.

Webb, Constance. *Richard Wright: A Biography*. New York: Putnam, 1968.

Also of Note

Richard Wright: Black Boy. Written, produced, and directed by Madison Davis Lacy; dramatic scenes directed by Horace Ové. Mississippi Educational Television/BBC production, 1995.